TRUTHS EVERY
CHRISTIAN
NEEDS TO KNOW

CLARENCE SEXTON

CROWN
CHRISTIAN
PUBLICATIONS
Royal Reading

Truths Every Christian Needs to Know

Clarence Sexton

Second Edition
Copyright
January 2004

CROWN
CHRISTIAN
PUBLICATIONS
Royal Reading

P.O. Box 159
Powell, Tennessee ◆ 37849
1-877 At-Crown
CrownChristianPublications.com
FaithfortheFamily.com

CHURCH PLANTING AND
SUNDAY SCHOOL SERIES

TRUTHS EVERY CHRISTIAN NEEDS TO KNOW

Second Edition

Copyright © 2004

Crown Christian Publications

Powell, Tennessee 37849

ISBN: 1-58981-192-5

Layout and design by Stephen Troell

Printed in the United States of America

DEDICATION

———◆◆◆———

PASTOR DILLARD HAGAN

———◆◆◆———

This book is affectionately dedicated to Pastor Dillard Hagan. When I was eighteen years old, God called me into the ministry. Pastor Hagan lovingly guided me, reproved me, corrected me, and instructed me in righteousness. He gave me my first opportunity to preach. He became my Paul, and I his Timothy. Because he taught me, I feel an accountability to God to *"teach others also."*

Clarence Sexton
Acts 5:42

TRUTHS EVERY CHRISTIAN NEEDS TO KNOW

PREFACE...9

INTRODUCTION: CHRIST DIED FOR US..11

CHAPTER ONE: THE BIRTHMARKS OF A BELIEVER.................................27

CHAPTER TWO: THE HOLY SCRIPTURES...41

CHAPTER THREE: GOD HEARS AND ANSWERS PRAYER..........................57

CHAPTER FOUR: WHAT THE BIBLE TEACHES ABOUT
the NEW TESTAMENT CHURCH......................................75

CHAPTER FIVE: HE THAT WINNETH SOULS IS WISE........................... 93

CHAPTER SIX: GIVING IS THE GOLDEN KEY
to GOD'S BLESSING...105

CHAPTER SEVEN: WE ARE COMMANDED TO BE
FILLED WITH THE HOLY SPIRIT................................127

CHAPTER EIGHT: THE LORD IS OUR GUIDE...147

CHAPTER NINE: WE ARE ENGAGED IN A SPIRITUAL WARFARE...............165

CHAPTER TEN: THE WORK OF THE LORD IS OUR MISSION................183

CHAPTER ELEVEN: THE COMING OF JESUS CHRIST
IS OUR BLESSED HOPE...201

CHAPTER TWELVE: WE MUST PREPARE FOR OUR DAY OF DEPARTURE...................219

CHAPTER THIRTEEN: GOD BEARS US ON EAGLES' WINGS.............................237

PREFACE

―・●・―

"ABLE TO TEACH OTHERS ALSO"

―・●・―

The Word of God says in II Timothy 2:2, *"And the things that thou hast heard of me among many witnesses, the same commit thou to faithful men, who shall be able to teach others also."* Many men and women have been used of God to teach me how to live for the Lord Jesus Christ. Because I *have*, I *owe* what has been given to me. God has designed His work to be done this way. Those who know the truth must commit it to others, and those who receive the truth must *"teach others also."* This is *the* principle to be followed in the work of the Lord.

Trusting the Lord Jesus Christ as your personal Savior is not an ending; it is only the beginning of all that God has for you. May God use this book to help you to be the Christian that He has saved you to be. As you receive the truth, you are responsible to *"teach others also."* Use what you find in this book to do just that!

Clarence Sexton

Acts 5:42

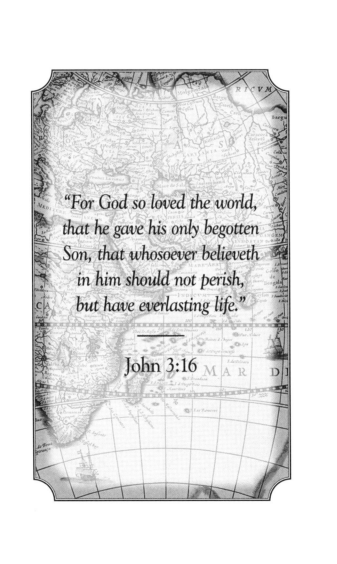

"For God so loved the world,
that he gave his only begotten
Son, that whosoever believeth
in him should not perish,
but have everlasting life."

———

John 3:16

CHRIST DIED FOR US

The Bible says in Psalm 89:47, *"Remember how short my time is."* In James 4:14, God's Word says that your life *"is even a vapour."* No matter how long we live, the Bible says that life *"is of few days"* (Job 14:1). After death, we go into eternity. The Lord has made a way for us to be with Him forever. This is why the Bible says in John 3:16, *"For God so loved the world, that he gave his only begotten Son, that whosoever believeth in him should not perish, but have everlasting life."*

A REAL HEAVEN

Heaven is a real place. The Lord Jesus said on one occasion,

> *Let not your heart be troubled: ye believe in God, believe also in me. In my Father's house*

> *are many mansions: if it were not so, I would*
> *have told you. I go to prepare a place for you.*
> *And if I go and prepare a place for you, I will*
> *come again, and receive you unto myself; that*
> *where I am, there ye may be also* (John 14:1-3).

One of Christ's disciples said, *"Lord, we know not whither thou goest; and how can we know the way?"* The Lord Jesus answered, *"I am the way, the truth, and the life: no man cometh unto the Father, but by me"* (John 14:5-6).

A Real Hell

If you believe what Christ said about heaven, you must realize that the Lord Jesus also said that there is a real hell. He spoke of a man who died and went to hell in Luke 16:23-24,

> *And in hell he lift up his eyes, being in torments,*
> *and seeth Abraham afar off, and Lazarus in his*
> *bosom. And he cried and said, Father Abraham,*
> *have mercy on me, and send Lazarus, that he may*
> *dip the tip of his finger in water, and cool my*
> *tongue; for I am tormented in this flame.*

If we are going to believe what Christ said about heaven, we should also believe what He said about hell. We were created for eternity, and every human being is going to live as long as God lives. Beyond the door of death, after our last breath here on earth, we are going to live forever somewhere. We will live either with God or without God.

Eternity Where?

Every human being has an appointment with death. After death, will you be in heaven or in hell? There is no question in life that deserves as much attention as this question. It is the one issue that must be settled. This is why, in John chapter three, the Lord Jesus said to a man who came to Him under the cover of darkness, *"Marvel not that I said unto thee, Ye must be born again"* (John 3:7).

Nicodemus was a very religious man, but he said to the Lord, "What do You mean? Must I go the second time into my mother's womb and come out again?" The Lord Jesus explained to him that men must have a spiritual birth.

ALL PEOPLE HAVE SINNED

We have all sinned, and we are dead in our sins. We must have a spiritual birth. In Romans 3:10 the Bible says, *"As it is written, There is none righteous, no, not one."*

In this chapter of the Bible, God lists what is wrong with humanity. He says,

> *There is none that understandeth, there is none that seeketh after God. They are all gone out of the way, they are together become unprofitable; there is none that doeth good, no, not one. Their throat is an open sepulchre; with their tongues they have used deceit; the poison of asps is under their lips: Whose mouth is full of cursing and bitterness: Their feet are swift to shed blood: Destruction and misery are in their ways: And the way of peace have they not known: There is no fear of God before their eyes. Now we know that what things soever the law saith, it saith to them who are under the law:*

that every mouth may be stopped, and all the world may become guilty before God. Therefore by the deeds of the law there shall no flesh be justified in his sight: for by the law is the knowledge of sin. But now the righteousness of God without the law is manifested, being witnessed by the law and the prophets; even the righteousness of God which is by faith of Jesus Christ unto all and upon all them that believe: for there is no difference (Romans 3:11-22).

The Lord speaks about Jews and Gentiles. He says, *"There is no difference."* When we come to verse twenty-three of Romans chapter three, He says, *"For all have sinned, and come short of the glory of God."* This means I am a sinner and you are a sinner. We are all sinners.

My wife grew up in the home of a Baptist preacher. Her father was killed in an automobile accident when she was only five years old. He was returning from a funeral home where he had gone to comfort a family that had suffered a death in their home. My wife, her brother, and her mother were at home in the kitchen making a cake to surprise him, but he never arrived.

My wife grew up in a fine Christian home. Her mother took her to church every Sunday morning, Sunday night, and Wednesday night. She talked to her about the Lord and salvation in Christ. My wife and I grew up very differently. My father was a professional gambler. No matter what our background is or what has happened in our lives, all of us have the same problem.

The problem with the world is not lying; it is what causes lying. The problem with the world is not immorality; it is what causes immorality. Each day five thousand people in America start using cocaine, but the problem is not drugs.

Terrible things are happening, and there is something behind it all. The thing behind it all is sin. We are all sinners. Our sin brings a high price. You may say, "I'm not a sinner." The Bible is true and it says, *"For all have sinned."* You may not think that you are as bad as someone you know personally, but we are all sinners.

The Bible says in Romans 6:23, *"For the wages of sin is death."* The payment or wages of our sin is death. This means death and hell. It means separation from God forever. We are born with a sin nature. In one sense, every human being is "still born" spiritually. We are spiritually dead.

Most people who are really busy trying to make the world a better place are only making it a better place from which to go to hell.

You may be trying to make the world a better place. I hope you are, but most people who are really busy trying to make the world a better place are only making it a better place from which to go to hell. We are going to live and die. Today, would it be heaven or hell for you?

CHRIST DIED FOR ALL PEOPLE

Let us remember that Christ died for our sins. All people are sinners in need of a Savior. Christ died for all, not just a few, but for all. In other words, I can go anywhere in the world and tell anyone I meet, "Jesus Christ died for you."

On every island of the sea, on every continent of the world, among every race, among every nationality, among every language group; people need to hear the Good News. The Good News is the gospel.

The apostle Paul wrote to the church in Corinth in I Corinthians 15:1-4,

> *Moreover, brethren, I declare unto you the gospel which I preached unto you, which also ye have received, and wherein ye stand; by which also ye are saved, if ye keep in memory what I preached unto you, unless ye have believed in vain. For I delivered unto you first of all that which I also received, how that Christ died for our sins according to the scriptures; and that he was buried, and that he rose again the third day according to the scriptures.*

We say this is the Good News. This is the gospel. All are sinners, but Christ died for our sins. This is good news, but only if one hears it before he dies. Let us thank God that we have heard it.

In Hebrews 2:9 the Bible says,

> *But we see Jesus, who was made a little lower than the angels for the suffering of death, crowned with glory and honour; that he by the grace of God should taste death for every man.*

I can look you in the face and say, "I have something very important to tell you. There is nothing more important to talk about. It is the only vital thing in life. Christ died for you. He died for all."

The most wonderful story anyone has ever heard is the story of Calvary and what Christ came to do on the cross. Most people can quote John 3:16, *"For God so loved the world, that he gave his only begotten Son, that whosoever believeth in him should not perish, but have everlasting life."* God loves you and loves me so much that He sent His Son to die on the cross for us.

Jesus Christ lived a sinless life. He was born of a virgin. He went about in His earthly ministry doing nothing but good. One night in a garden He was praying. He was not praying with His hands neatly clasped, kneeling at a stone as some artist might paint; but the Bible says He was on His face in the dirt, and great sweat drops of blood broke through the pores of His flesh.

The most wonderful story anyone has ever heard is the story of Calvary and what Christ came to do on the cross.

He prayed under the agony of our sin, not His own, as He was about to go to the cross to bleed and die for us. From the hillside, coming down across the Kedron brook with torches and lanterns, a band of men came to take Christ. They brought lanterns and torches because they thought they would have to chase Him into some cave or some place where He would go to hide. But when they came to Him, He stepped out to meet them.

I have stood in that garden in the land of the Bible many times, thinking how He could have seen them coming. If He had wanted to run, He could have; but He did not run. The Bible says that He stepped forth. When they inquired about who He was, He spoke, *"I am."* When He said those words, the men who came to take Him fell to the ground.

Think of how hardened people's hearts can become. Can you imagine this mob coming to take Christ? After hearing the sound of His voice, they actually fell to the ground. Yet they got up and continued toward Him.

No doubt they thought as they bound His hands that Christ would be unwilling. He was not unwilling. He freely offered Himself. He gave His life. The Lord Jesus said, *"No man taketh it from me, but I lay it down of myself"* (John 10:18).

The Lord Jesus and His disciples had a discussion earlier about carrying swords. The Bible says they had two swords. I do not know exactly why this is mentioned in the Bible, but they had two swords among them. Peter had one of them.

"No man taketh it from me, but I lay it down of myself."

The high priest's servant, a man by the name of Malchus, started to bind the hands of the Lord Jesus. Peter could not stand it any longer. He drew his sword and went for the man's head. He missed his head and cut off the man's ear. His ear fell to the ground.

If you have ever had a wound on your face, you know that it bleeds profusely. No doubt, blood was pouring. Christ took Malchus' ear and reattached it to his head in the presence of all the witnesses, but they still took Him. Christ went through a mockery trial that night and was delivered the next morning to Pilate. From Pilate, He was taken to Herod, and then back to Pilate.

Someone said, "He's a king," so they crowned Him with thorns and pressed them deep into His brow. They said, "He's a king, let's anoint Him." So they spat on His face until His face

CHRIST DIED FOR US

was covered with spittle. They said, "He's a king, let's put a robe on Him," and they placed a robe of mockery on His shoulders after they had beaten His back until it was broken and bleeding. Eventually they brought Him before a mob of angry people, and the mob cried out, "Release Barabbas and crucify Christ."

Christ bore the cross to Calvary. When He came to the place of crucifixion, they took spikes and drove them into His hands and feet, lifting Him up on a cross between heaven and hell; and there He hung.

If you see Him in your mind's eye, you ask, "Why? He never sinned. Why? He never did anything wrong. Why? They lied about Him. False witnesses came to testify against Him. He was the only innocent One who ever walked the earth, yet He hung there and bled and died."

The people heard Him cry out, *"My God, my God, why hast thou forsaken me?"* The billows of God's wrath rolled over the Lord Jesus as He became sin for us. God's Word says in II Corinthians 5:21, *"For he hath made him to be sin for us, who knew no sin; that we might be made the righteousness of God in him."*

> *The billows of God's wrath rolled over the Lord Jesus as He became sin for us.*

Christ bled and died for the sin debt of the whole world. We do not get the picture when we say "the whole world." We do not quite understand when we think about the billions of people alive today and the millions who have lived before us. We might, however, get the picture when we say, "He died for me."

What do you think about what Christ did for you? How are you going to respond to what Christ did for you? I am God's messenger to tell you that Jesus Christ loves you and that He died for you. He was buried and rose from the dead. He came bodily out of the grave. The stone that covered the tomb where His body was placed was rolled away; not so Christ could get out, but so others could go in and identify that the tomb was empty. Because of His resurrection, we have hope.

Christ said, *"I am the resurrection, and the life: he that believeth in me, though he were dead, yet shall he live: and whosoever liveth and believeth in me shall never die"* (John 11:25-26).

Christ asked the sister of Lazarus, *"Believest thou this?"* She said, *"Yea, Lord."* I want to stand beside her and shout, "Yes, Lord, I believe also!" Do you believe?

ALL PEOPLE ARE SAVED THE SAME WAY

Everyone comes to God the same way. I am not going to heaven because I am a minister. I am not going to heaven because someone felt sorry for me. My wife is not going to heaven because her daddy was a preacher. All people are saved the same way.

Let us consider an interesting verse that most people do not understand, but it explains the whole matter. In Romans 3:26 the Bible says, *"To declare, I say, at this time his righteousness: that he might be just, and the justifier of him which believeth in Jesus."* God is just, and He is the Justifier.

How can a holy God allow sinful creatures into heaven and still say that He is a just God? He is just, and He is the Justifier. The Bible teaches that when we come to Christ and trust Him as our Savior, God declares that we are justified. Some think that being justified means "just as if we had never sinned." I appreciate that thought, but it means so much more than that. It means more than being regarded just as if I had never sinned. It means to be regarded by God just as if I were never a sinner. There is a great difference.

I love to talk about my grandchildren. I want my grandchildren to go to heaven. I want to be there with them some day. I love them. I am enjoying them here, but I want to be in heaven with them. I do not want to go to heaven without my family.

Some people have grandchildren who are going to heaven, but they are not going to heaven with their grandchildren. Let us get the entire family to Christ for salvation.

When my sons did something wrong while growing up, I forgave them. I forgave them just as they had forgiven me of things, but I could not erase what they did.

For the child of God, our heavenly Father not only forgives us; He erases any record of what we have done. There is no record that we were ever sinners. When one asks God to forgive his sin and places his faith in Christ as his Savior, God declares his sin paid for on the cross. He imputes or puts Christ's record on the Christian's account. He sees His children as He sees Christ.

Being justified means to be regarded by God just as if I were never a sinner.

Christ was never a sinner. It is more than the fact that He never sinned. He was never a sinner. When God looks at our record, He sees Christ's record on our account just as if we had never been sinners.

The Devil is doing a terrible work. But the work that God does through Christ is a greater work than what the Devil does through his evil efforts. God's work is greater than the Devil's. The Devil's work can be undone. Christ's work can never be undone. We are all children of the Devil by nature. We have all sinned *"and come short of the glory of God."*

Every human being is already under a death sentence. God has held court and declared, "The whole world is guilty. The world is sentenced to go to hell forever without God and without hope."

Our lovely Savior, Jesus Christ, came to this earth, bled and died on the cross, and paid our sin debt so we would not have to go to hell without God and without hope. He was buried and He rose from the dead that first Easter morning. When we ask the Lord to forgive our sin and by faith trust Christ as Savior, He hears our prayer, forgives our sin, and saves us.

You may say, "I believe all of this." Do you? The Bible says, *"For by grace are ye saved through faith; and that not of yourselves: it is the gift of God: Not of works, lest any man should boast"* (Ephesians 2:8-9).

There are many people who believe that they are sinners and that Christ died for their sin, but they have never trusted Christ and Christ alone for their soul's salvation. Many people believe in Christ plus baptism, Christ plus good works, Christ plus first communion, or Christ plus the Lord's Supper. The Bible teaches that salvation is not by any work that we have done. It is by Christ and Christ alone. No man can earn his way into heaven.

Charles Spurgeon, a preacher of a century ago, said, "If I got to heaven because of my good works; when I walked into heaven through a gate of pearl, onto a street of gold, and saw mansions of glory, I would say, 'Oh Lord, I don't deserve to be here!' But if I get there because of what Jesus Christ has done, I am going to walk through that gate of pearl and say, 'Oh, how wonderful is this place, and I expected such a work that only Christ could do.'"

No man can earn his way into heaven.

You ask, "What must I do?"

Allow me to tell you my story. When I was a teenage boy, I went to a youth choir practice at my local church. The choir director said to me, "I would like for you to stay behind because I want to talk to you." He asked, "Clarence, are you a Christian?" He knew a bit about my home life, and he was troubled about some of those things.

I said, "I guess I am. I'm not a heathen. I go to Sunday School and church. I have a Bible."

He understood what I was missing. He explained to me what I have written to you. He took me down the hallway from the choir room into the pastor's office, and he and the pastor sat across from me. They asked me if I would pray from my heart and trust Christ and Christ alone, ask God to forgive my sin, acknowledge to God that I was sinner, and invite the Lord Jesus into my life as my Savior.

I did not know how to pray, but these men led me in a prayer. I knew prayers like,

> Now I lay me down to sleep,
> I pray the Lord my soul to keep.
> If I should die before I wake,
> I pray the Lord my soul to take.

But I did not know how to pray to become a Christian. They led me in a prayer to God for salvation.

That day, I did not trust myself or trust them. I trusted in Christ alone, because all are saved the same way. I asked God to forgive my sin, and I received Jesus Christ as my Savior. Bells did not ring. Lights did not flash. I did not feel funny all over. I knew that I had taken God at His Word and trusted the Lord Jesus as my Savior.

For example, a chair will support my weight; but it will not actually support me until I trust it to do so. You can say what you will about God, about Christ, about His saving power, but He is not your personal Savior until you trust Christ and Christ alone to save you.

Some day, I know I will be in heaven with God. What a wonderful thing it would be if you were there also. The only way you will be there is if you personally trust Christ for your soul's salvation.

Let us review what God says in His Word about salvation. All have sinned. Christ died for all people. All are saved the same way. If you have not already trusted Christ to be your Savior, pray and receive Christ as your Savior today. You may pray from your heart this prayer to God:

> Lord Jesus, I know that I am a sinner. I know that You died for my sins and that You rose from the dead. Forgive my sin and come into my life. I trust You as my personal Savior. Now help me live for You from this day forward. In Jesus' name, Amen.

Please write me and let me know if you have prayed and received the Lord Jesus Christ as your Savior as a result of reading this. I pray that the things you read in the remainder of this book will help you in your new life as a Christian.

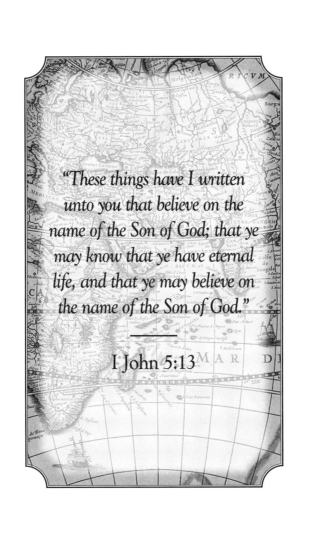

"These things have I written unto you that believe on the name of the Son of God; that ye may know that ye have eternal life, and that ye may believe on the name of the Son of God."

———

I John 5:13

CHAPTER ONE

THE BIRTHMARKS OF A BELIEVER

The Bible says in I John 5:13, *"These things have I written unto you that believe on the name of the Son of God; that ye may know that ye have eternal life, and that ye may believe on the name of the Son of God."*

What a tragic thing it is to go through this life uncertain of where you will be for all eternity. If you know the Lord and believe the Bible, you can know for sure that heaven is your home.

Once you have eternal life, it is a present possession never to be taken away. If it were not eternal life, if it were not everlasting life, it would be called something else. But God says that we can know that we have *eternal* life.

All sixty-six books of the Bible have a specific purpose. The purpose of each book complements the purpose of the entire Book. If you had a puzzle with sixty-six pieces in it and you removed one of the pieces of the puzzle, you would have an incomplete puzzle. If you remove one of the sixty-six books in the Bible, you have an incomplete Book. We need to know the message of each of the sixty-six books and allow God to use the message of each book to speak to our hearts and complete us in Christ, to make us the people that God intends for us to be.

This record of our Lord Jesus Christ is written so that people might believe on Him.

John the apostle, the beloved disciple of our Lord, was the human penman for five books of the Bible–the Gospel according to John, I John, II John, III John, and the book of the Revelation of Jesus Christ.

In John 20:31 the Bible says, *"But these are written, that ye might believe that Jesus is the Christ, the Son of God; and that believing ye might have life through his name."*

This verse of Scripture in John 20:31 leaves no room for doubt about why the Gospel record of John is given. It is written so that people *"might believe that Jesus is the Christ, the Son of God; and that believing they might have life through his name."* This record of our Lord Jesus Christ is written so that people might believe on Him.

When we look back at I John 5:13, this book of the Bible says of itself, *"These things have I written unto you that believe."* John is writing to those who already believe.

John 20:31 says that the Gospel according to John was written *"that ye might believe."* But I John 5:13 is written to those who already believe that they may know that they have eternal life. Each book has its purpose.

Let us work our way from the beginning of the book of I John to see the purpose of this book.

TO PROMOTE JOY IN OUR LIVES

In I John 1:4, God says that He gives us this book to promote joy in our lives. *"And these things write we unto you, that your joy may be full."* Do you have that joy?

TO PREVENT SIN

The Word of God says that God has given us this book of the Bible to prevent sin. I John 2:1 says, *"My little children, these things write I unto you, that ye sin not."* Christians are not sinless, but they should sin less.

If one is a believer, there should be certain birthmarks in his life.

TO PROTECT THE SAINTS

This little book of the Bible is given to us to protect the saints. I John 2:26 says, *"These things have I written unto you concerning them that seduce you."*

TO PROVIDE ASSURANCE

I John 5:13 tells us that this book of the Bible is given to provide assurance. The Bible says, *"These things have I written unto you that believe on the name of the Son of God; that ye may know that ye have eternal life."*

Let us consider "The Birthmarks of a Believer." If one is a believer, there should be certain birthmarks in his life.

There are certain evidences of children that cause them to be identified with their parents. I was in the store with my oldest son recently and a lady said, "I see the resemblance." I knew, of course, what she was talking about. She thought my son favored his father.

> *Not everyone who says he or she is a Christian is a Christian.*

If you are a child of God, there are certain birthmarks that should be easy to find in your life. These birthmarks should identify you with your heavenly Father. This does not mean you must have those marks in order to become a Christian, but rather that they give evidence that you are a Christian.

Not everyone who says he or she is a Christian is a Christian. Let us see what the Bible says about this. In I John 2:19 the Bible says,

> *They went out from us, but they were not of us; for if they had been of us, they would no doubt have continued with us: but they went out, that they might be made manifest that they were not all of us.*

There are many people who identify with Jesus Christ as Christians. Some are very winsome, like Judas. Judas was the man who carried the money bag. Only the best guy would have been chosen to do that.

Can you imagine the most trustworthy of the disciples, the fellow who at least appeared to be the most trustworthy, turned out to be the one who was not really a believer at all?

Allow God's Word to speak to your heart and see if these birthmarks of a believer are evident in your life.

THE BIRTHMARK OF OBEDIENCE

The first birthmark is the birthmark of obedience. Do you have it? Do you have an obedient heart? Obedience is not simply doing the will of God; it is delighting in doing the will of God. Obedience is a wonderful birthmark.

There are many people who say they are Christians but have no desire to obey the Lord. They lack evidence in their Christian lives. Do you have the birthmark of obedience in your life?

I John 2:3-6 says,

> *And hereby we do know that we know him, if we keep his commandments. He that saith, I know him, and keepeth not his commandments, is a liar, and the truth is not in him. But whoso keepeth his word, in him verily is the love of God perfected: hereby know we that we are in him. He that saith he abideth in him ought himself also so to walk, even as he walked.*

Do you ever stop to think how many people are counting on some religious experience to get them to heaven but have no real steadfast assurance? They are holding to some fragment of religion. May the Spirit of God speak to each of us and reveal whether or not we have this birthmark of a believer–the birthmark of obedience to God.

THE BIRTHMARK OF LOVE

The second birthmark is the birthmark of love. I John 3:14-19 says,

> *We know that we have passed from death unto life, because we love the brethren. He that loveth not his brother abideth in death. Whosoever*

hateth his brother is a murderer: and ye know that no murderer hath eternal life abiding in him. Hereby perceive we the love of God, because he laid down his life for us: and we ought to lay down our lives for the brethren. But whoso hath this world's good, and seeth his brother have need, and shutteth up his bowels of compassion from him, how dwelleth the love of God in him? My little children, let us not love in word, neither in tongue; but in deed and in truth. And hereby we know that we are of the truth, and shall assure our hearts before him.

Some people are kinder than other people. Some people have more winsome personalities than other people. Some people are more approachable than other people. But here God talks about loving others with the love of Christ.

Have you come to realize that all we have is not ours to keep but ours for God to use at His bidding?

If you are thinking, "I'm a very caring, loving person," do you love those who do not love you? How do you speak about those who do not love you? Do you use the means God has placed at your disposal to be a blessing to others? Have you come to realize that all we have is not ours to keep but ours for God to use at His bidding?

Love is not a word; love is a deed. It is a commitment. It is one of the identifying birthmarks of a believer.

THE BIRTHMARK OF TRUTH

The third birthmark is the birthmark of truth. I John 4:1-6 says,

> *Beloved, believe not every spirit, but try the spirits whether they are of God: because many false prophets are gone out into the world. Hereby know ye the Spirit of God: every spirit that confesseth that Jesus Christ is come in the flesh is of God: and every spirit that confesseth not that Jesus Christ is come in the flesh is not of God: and this is that spirit of antichrist, whereof ye have heard that it should come; and even now already is it in the world. Ye are of God, little children, and have overcome them: because greater is he that is in you, than he that is in the world. They are of the world: therefore speak they of the world, and the world heareth them. We are of God: he that knoweth God heareth us; he that is not of God heareth not us. Hereby know we the spirit of truth, and the spirit of error.*

If there has ever been a day when people want to talk about God without talking about the Lord Jesus Christ being God, this is the day. Almost everyone talks about God. They say, "We need to trust God. We need God in our lives.We need to pray to God."

If you are a Christian, do not express yourself this way. Use the title, "The Lord Jesus Christ." Express your faith in Christ. Pray in the name of the Lord Jesus Christ.

No doubt there are many people who are Christians, but are timid and disobedient to God. Many write books, offer prayers, and speak in public meetings; they talk about God, but they are afraid of offending someone and avoid saying, "The Lord Jesus Christ."

Are these people saved? Let the Spirit of God work on their hearts. But let us be clearly identified by the birthmark of the truth concerning the Lord Jesus Christ.

Some of us do not deny Him in word, but we deny Him in deed. Some of us do not deny Him with our lips, but we deny Him with our lives. Our behavior betrays the fact that we are Christians. This is not the way Christ would respond. This is not the way Christ would behave or speak. Do you and I have the birthmark of truth in our lives?

THE BIRTHMARK OF THE HOLY SPIRIT

The fourth birthmark is the birthmark of the Holy Spirit. In I John 4:13 the Bible says, *"Hereby know we that we dwell in him, and he in us, because he hath given us of his Spirit."*

Let us not make more or less of this than what God says here. The Holy Spirit is a Person. Just like you know people in your life and you can call them by name and you can get well acquainted with some of them, we need to be acquainted with the Person of the Holy Spirit.

Do you know the Holy Spirit? This is a birthmark of the believer. His indwelling presence is a birthmark of the true believer.

There are other religions and other people who talk about God and talk about religious experiences. But they do not talk about the power of the indwelling Holy Spirit to enable them to live the Christian life. They do not talk about being filled with the Holy Spirit. They know nothing of being baptized by the Spirit of God into the body of Christ at the moment of salvation. They know nothing of a spiritual anointing by the Holy Spirit to do the work of God. They do not talk about the earnest of the Holy Spirit as He comes to abide in the believer forever.

This birthmark can be witnessed by others who are believers. Have you spoken to people at times and talked about the things of God, and you have not only met that person, but you have met the Holy Spirit in that person? Have there been times you have met people and talked with them and they talked about religion, but there was no meeting of the Holy Spirit in them?

I have met people thousands of miles from home on different continents of the world and have begun to talk to them about Jesus Christ, and I have sensed the witness of the Holy Spirit. I did not know them, but I knew the Holy Spirit. I had never met them before, but I surely knew the Holy Spirit. I had never seen them before in my life, but I surely knew the Holy Spirit when I met Him.

There are other spirits, but there is only one Holy Spirit who is coequal, coexistent, eternally existent with God the Father and God the Son. This is the Holy Spirit, who is God. We should know Him. This is a birthmark of a believer. I John 4:13 says, *"Hereby know we that we dwell in him, and he in us, because he hath given us of his Spirit."*

THE BIRTHMARK OF THE WITNESS WITHIN

The fifth birthmark is the birthmark of the witness within. Consider I John 5:9-13,

> *If we receive the witness of men, the witness of God is greater: for this is the witness of God which he hath testified of his Son. He that believeth on the Son of God hath the witness in*

himself: he that believeth not God hath made him a liar; because he believeth not the record that God gave of his Son. And this is the record, that God hath given to us eternal life, and this life is in his Son. He that hath the Son hath life; and he that hath not the Son of God hath not life. These things have I written unto you that believe on the name of the Son of God; that ye may know that ye have eternal life, and that ye may believe on the name of the Son of God.

When we trust the Lord Jesus as our personal Savior, the Holy Spirit comes to abide in us. He becomes our witness within. The Bible says, *"Christ in you, the hope of glory"* (Colossians 1:27). The Lord lives in each believer and provides assurance that we are His through this divine witness.

When dealing with people about what we refer to as the "assurance of their salvation," many of us take them immediately to I John 5:13 and say to them, "You can know for sure."

Is this not what the Bible says? Sure, it is. It says, *"These things have I written unto you that believe on the name of the Son of God; that ye may know that ye have eternal life, and that ye may believe on the name of the Son of God."*

Yes, we can know, but we are taking the verse completely out of context. Notice the expression, *"these things."* What are *"these things"*?

It does not say, "This verse is written." The Bible does not say, "This verse is written unto you that believe on the name of the Son of God; that ye may know..." But this is the way we read it.

We read it and try to use it as if it says, "This verse is written." But it does not say, "This verse is written." It says, *"These things have I written..."* It summarizes the entire book.

You may have a profession of faith. You may know the Lord as your Savior. But you are not going to live in the joy of assurance of the present possession you have in Christ Jesus unless these things, these birthmarks, are found in your life.

Let us review. The birthmark of obedience is found in I John 2:3-6. The birthmark of love is found in I John 3:14-19. The birthmark of truth is found in I John 4:1-6. The birthmark of the Holy Spirit is found in I John 4:13. The birthmark of the witness within is found in I John 5:9-13. If these five things God clearly points out in His Word are in your life, then God says, *"These things have I written unto you that believe on the name of the Son of God; that ye may know that ye have eternal life."*

You are not going to live in the joy of assurance of the present possession you have in Christ Jesus unless these things, these birthmarks, are found in your life.

I have answers to prayer and many things other than the day I trusted Christ as my Savior to be able to testify about the assurance I have in Christ. You may say, "There was a time when I asked God to forgive my sin and by faith I trusted Christ as my Savior." This is wonderful. Salvation is instantaneous. The Lord comes to live in your life. He quickens you from the dead. That moment, you are regenerated as you trust Christ as Savior, repenting of your sin, and by faith trusting Christ and Christ alone. God makes Himself known to you. He reveals His Son to you and He comes to live in your life.

When the Samaritan woman in John chapter four wanted to know the Messiah, the Lord Jesus said, *"I that speak unto thee am he"* (John 4:26). At that moment, He made Himself known to her.

There was a moment when you desired to know Christ. You asked God to forgive your sin. Your heart was convicted and drawn by the Spirit of God. At that moment, you wanted to know the Lord. He made Himself known to you. But how do you have this assurance? You can have this assurance by having these birthmarks in your life–the birthmarks of obedience, love, truth, the Holy Spirit, and the witness within.

TRUTHS TO REMEMBER

Every believer is to have an obedient heart toward the Lord Jesus Christ (I John 2:3-6).

Children of God are to love others with the love of Christ (I John 3:14-19).

Christians should clearly identify with the Lord Jesus Christ both in word and deed (I John 4:1-6).

When someone trusts the Lord Jesus as personal Savior, the Holy Spirit comes to abide in him forever (I John 4:13; John 14:16-17).

The power of the indwelling Holy Spirit enables God's children to live the Christian life (I John 4:4; Ephesians 5:18).

Every Christian can have assurance of salvation by having the birthmarks of a believer in his life (I John 5:13).

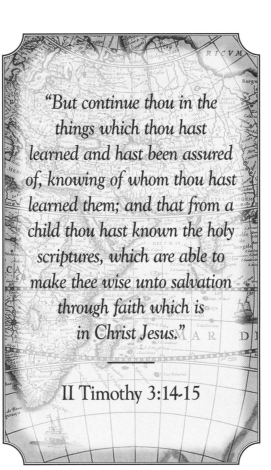

"But continue thou in the things which thou hast learned and hast been assured of, knowing of whom thou hast learned them; and that from a child thou hast known the holy scriptures, which are able to make thee wise unto salvation through faith which is in Christ Jesus."

II Timothy 3:14-15

CHAPTER TWO

THE HOLY SCRIPTURES

e are living in perilous times, in an increasingly unhappy world. The further people move from God and God's Word, the more miserable they are going to be.

People are trying every vanity in this world to gain happiness, plunging in again and again and coming up empty. They are *"ever learning, and never able to come to the knowledge of the truth"* (II Timothy 3:7). There is no true fulfillment outside of knowing Jesus Christ and living a life of obedience to Him.

The Bible says in II Timothy 3:13-17,

> *But evil men and seducers shall wax worse and worse, deceiving, and being deceived. But continue thou in the things which thou hast learned and hast been assured of, knowing of whom thou hast learned them; and that from a*

child thou hast known the holy scriptures, which are able to make thee wise unto salvation through faith which is in Christ Jesus. All scripture is given by inspiration of God, and is profitable for doctrine, for reproof, for correction, for instruction in righteousness: that the man of God may be perfect, throughly furnished unto all good works.

The term *"holy scriptures"* is used in reference to the Bible. The word *"scriptures"* means "writings." These are not just writings; these are the holy writings of God. When we hold the Bible in our hands, we are holding the Holy Scriptures.

These are not just writings; these are the holy writings of God.

We find an amazing truth about these Holy Scriptures in Psalm 119:89. The Bible says, *"For ever, O LORD, thy word is settled in heaven."* Before any word of the Bible was ever given to men to pen, every word of the Bible was settled in heaven forever. When God says *"for ever,"* that is what He means. *"For ever, O LORD, thy word is settled in heaven."*

In Psalm 119:152 the Bible says, *"Concerning thy testimonies, I have known of old that thou hast founded them for ever."* We are able to hold in our hands and hide in our hearts the only eternal thing the human eye will ever look upon.

In II Timothy chapter three, God's Word deals with the subject of *"perilous times."* The chapter begins, *"This know also, that in the last days perilous times shall come."* Then, in verses two through five, a list is given of things that characterize these perilous times.

For men shall be lovers of their own selves, covetous, boasters, proud, blasphemers, disobedient to parents, unthankful, unholy, without natural affection, trucebreakers, false accusers, incontinent, fierce, despisers of those that are good, traitors, heady, highminded, lovers of pleasures more than lovers of God; having a form of godliness, but denying the power thereof: from such turn away.

What a list! Paul says, *"Having a form of godliness."* The most dangerous error is the error that attempts to disguise itself in the garments of religion. These risky or perilous times bring to the forefront *"a form of godliness"* that is not of God.

The most dangerous error is the error that attempts to disguise itself in the garments of religion.

Have all these things existed in every civilization? Certainly they have, but they are completely characteristic of our age. They have been woven into the fabric of our times. Worldwide, these things characterize our day.

On the list is the word *"incontinent."* This word means "falling apart; being torn apart; coming apart." We are living in a world that is literally breaking apart.

The word *"fierce"* means "savagely violent." Many are filled with fear. The Bible says the terrible thing about all of this is that *"evil men and seducers shall wax worse and worse."* But we are not to bury our heads in the sand.

We have an understanding of the times in which we live. We are not to be frightened because *"For God hath not given us the spirit of fear; but of power, and of love, and of a sound mind"* (II Timothy 1:7).

So what are we to do? We are to do exactly what we find in the Bible. God takes us directly to His Word. In these perilous times, He takes us to the Holy Scriptures.

The Bible says for us to continue in the things we have been assured of, *"But continue thou in the things which thou hast learned and hast been assured of, knowing of whom thou hast learned them; and that from a child thou hast known the holy scriptures"* (II Timothy 3:14-15). There is a work that only the Word of God can accomplish.

I can remember when I received my first Bible. When I was nine years old, while visiting the doctor, I received an invitation to go to Sunday School. The pediatrician was a Sunday School teacher, and he invited my mother to bring me to his class. My mother made sure I got there. When I got to his class, he gave me a little Bible. I still have that Bible.

I knew that Bible was important, and I knew that it was a precious Book when I received it. But with every passing year, I realize more and more how precious the Bible truly is. It is an anchor for our souls. It is God's fixed point of reference in a world that is always changing. To our shame, there is nothing in human life so valuable yet so neglected as the Bible. It is available to us, but we do not make ourselves available to God's Word.

Every Christian should spend time in God's Word each day. We should read a passage from the Bible and let God speak to us. We should search God's Word, comparing Scripture with Scripture. We also need to meditate on Scripture and memorize Scripture, so that we might hide God's Word in our hearts.

Everything we see around us should be judged through scriptural eyes. We should not look at the world to interpret the Bible; we should search the Scriptures to interpret what is going on in the world. It is impossible to be spiritual without being scriptural. Let us determine to live by the clear teaching of the Bible.

THE INSPIRATION OF ALL SCRIPTURE

When attempting to speak the truth, it is always better to use the very language of the Bible if at all possible. Fix in your mind the language of the Bible, *"All scripture is given by inspiration of God."* Many people say that only certain parts of the Bible are inspired and that they happen to be inspired to tell us which parts. Let there be no confusion in this vital matter— *"All scripture is given by inspiration of God."*

Often when people are talking about the Bible and the human instrumentality God used to pen the Bible, they speak of the writers being inspired. However, the inspiration of Scripture is not referring to the inspiration of the writers, but to the writings. God revealed His words to men.

There are those who tell us that God inspired the thoughts, leaving the writers of Scripture free to clothe those thoughts in their own words. This thinking can easily lead to the belief that the Bible merely contains the Word of God. The amazing thing about this is that it is exactly the opposite of the truth.

If we believe the testimony of the Scripture, we must say that God always gave the words but did not always reveal the thoughts to the writers. This is made perfectly clear by certain passages of Scripture.

For example, in I Peter 1:10-11 the Bible says,

> *Of which salvation the prophets have inquired and searched diligently, who prophesied of the grace that should come unto you: searching what, or what manner of time the Spirit of Christ which was in them did signify, when it testified beforehand the sufferings of Christ, and the glory that should follow.*

In this passage we see that when the prophets wrote of Christ, they actually had to study the prophecies they themselves had written, and even then, they did not fully understand what they had written.

In Daniel 12:8-9 the Bible says, *"And I heard, but I understood not: then said I, O my Lord, what shall be the end of these things? And he said, Go thy way, Daniel: for the words are closed up and sealed till the time of the end."*

Here we find Daniel writing words given to him by divine inspiration which Daniel himself could not understand. He had to think about what he had written. Though God gave him the very words to write, the Bible says he *"understood not."*

The spade of the archeologist has never unearthed anything that has disproved the inspiration of Scripture. The Scriptures themselves testify of divine inspiration, and of course the testimony of the Lord Jesus Christ gives witness to the inspiration of Scripture. *"All scripture is given by inspiration of God."*

The Bible is a true record because it is God-breathed, and God cannot lie. When the Devil gives directives, do not listen to him; he is a liar. For example, he told Eve she would not die— he lied. Though the Bible records this statement given by Satan which is not the truth, it is a true record of the statement being made by the Devil. We must know who is speaking and to whom God's Word is speaking, because everything in the Bible is a true record. It is God's Word.

Taking verses out of context has caused grave errors, and if one does that, he can prove almost anything he desires to prove. I can tell you that it is right to go out and hang yourself if I take out of context the story of Judas Iscariot hanging himself. No, the Bible does not say to go out and hang yourself. But God gives us a true record of what Judas Iscariot did. After he betrayed Christ, he went out and hanged himself.

The entire Bible is God-breathed. Consider the words of Jesus Christ in Matthew 4:4. When our Lord was being tempted by the Devil, He defeated the Devil with the Word of God. The Bible says, *"But he answered and said, It is written, Man shall not live by bread alone, but by every word that proceedeth out of the mouth of God."* This is a wonderful description of inspiration given by our Savior, *"every word that proceedeth out of the mouth of God."*

God only wrote one Book. As you hold the Bible in your hands, you have the one Book God wrote.

God only wrote one Book. As you hold the Bible in your hands, you have the one Book God wrote. Can you imagine that the Creator God who made you and spoke the world into existence, our all-wise God, our Almighty God, the God before whom we shall stand some day, has written a Book? Every word of that Book was settled before any word of it was ever given to men to pen. Every word of it came from the very mouth of God.

May God illuminate our minds and teach us the doctrine of inspiration. *"All scripture is given by inspiration of God."*

THE NECESSITY OF ALL SCRIPTURE

Let us place emphasis on all Scripture. This is a neglected truth. The Bible says in II Timothy 3:16, *"All scripture is given by inspiration of God."*

When speaking of the necessity of Scripture, we get the idea that we are dealing with Scripture in general. But if we emphasize the necessity of all Scripture, we must also consider the Scriptures specifically. We need to realize the necessity of every book of the Bible and every chapter in every book of the Bible. Most Christians are only familiar with parts of the Bible. They may be extremely familiar with certain parts of the Bible, but very few Christians are familiar with *"all scripture."*

In a puzzle, all pieces are necessary to complete the whole. The puzzle is incomplete if any piece is missing, even if it is a very small piece.

The Bible is a Book of sixty-six books. Each book is necessary to complete the whole. Each book has a specific message that is a part of the big picture of the entire Book.

It is our Lord's desire to complete His children. Each message from each book is necessary to accomplish this goal. No book can be overlooked. If the message of one book is neglected in our lives, we cannot have all God desires for us. If you took one book out of the Bible, it would not be complete. If you took out Obadiah or Joel or Habakkuk or Philemon, the Bible would not be complete.

When God breathed these words for men to pen, He gave every book for a purpose. In every book of the Bible, God has a specific message for His children. The sixty-six books are all necessary to complete the message of God to men.

What has the book of Joel said to you as a child of God? What has the book of Obadiah said to you? What has God said to you through the book of Habakkuk? What has God said to you through the book of Leviticus? What has God said to you through the book of Jude? What has God said to you through the book of Romans? What has God said to you through the book of Judges? What has God said to you through the book of Lamentations? Immediately all of us are quite ashamed because we are not familiar with some of these books of the Bible.

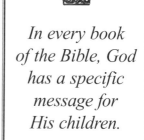

In every book of the Bible, God has a specific message for His children.

God gave us sixty-six books in this one Book because the message of each book is necessary. If we remove the message of any one of these books, then there is something incomplete about all that God wants us to know. Every one of God's children should read the Bible, search the Scriptures, meditate on the Scriptures, memorize Scriptures, and ask God by His Spirit to teach him the message of each book of the Bible. Most Christians are traveling through this world spending very little time with the message God has for each of us.

At times I do a mental exercise, visualizing the entire Bible. I visualize each book of the Bible, from the book of Genesis all the way through the Old and New Testaments. I try to recall, without looking at my Bible, everything I know about each book of the Bible. I find myself walking through the Bible.

I recall every character I know from each book. As I meet people from each book in the hallway of my mind, I rehearse everything I know about each person. Then I go back and trace each event I can recall. This process does not take long, but I want to use my mind to know God's Word. I think of the favorite passages that God has used to speak to my heart.

Many of us can shout and say, "Amen!" to the truth of the inspiration of all Scripture, but how convicting it is to consider the necessity of all Scripture. If we really believe in the necessity of all Scripture, then we should not be neglecting any Scripture. Our lives are incomplete without God's message from each book of the Bible.

Imagine the certain pieces of clothing that are worn to get dressed. It takes every piece of clothing to be properly attired. If I take a piece of that clothing out of my daily wardrobe, then I am not properly attired; something is missing.

God uses all of His Word to make us complete in Him.

When God gave us sixty-six books of the Bible, He gave us each book to help us be the children of God He desires for us to be. Without having all these books of the Bible and the message of each of these books, we miss much of what God has for us. Often we speak of having a balanced life. Let us change the word to *complete*—complete in Christ. God uses all of His Word to make us complete in Him. The Holy Scriptures are all inspired and all necessary.

THE SUFFICIENCY OF ALL SCRIPTURE

We know that Christ is all–sufficient. The Bible tells us our sufficiency is of God. *"For in him dwelleth all the fulness of the Godhead bodily"* (Colossians 2:9). He is enough; He is everything we need. We should not say that we believe in the all–sufficient Savior without saying we believe in the all–sufficient Scriptures.

God has told us from His Word that He knows what is in man (John 2:25). I do not know about men by studying men; I know about men by knowing God. He created men.

If you have a problem with your children, you do not need to know more about your children; you need to know more of God who made your children and gave them to you. He will reveal to you how you are to deal with your children. He teaches us through His all–sufficient Word.

The Bible declares that we are to live with our wives *"according to knowledge"* (I Peter 3:7). We are to know them. How can we know them? If we know God better, God will teach us. He made our wives. He will teach us how we are to love them and treat them. He knows what is in them.

Declaring that the Scriptures are all–sufficient is declaring that God's Word meets every need. Go to God's Word with your needs.

The Lord gives us insight in II Timothy 3:15, *"And that from a child thou hast known the holy scriptures, which are able to make thee wise unto salvation through faith which is in Christ Jesus."* The greatest need we have is salvation, and the first thing God says in this passage about His Word is that it makes us *"wise unto salvation."* We must know how to have our sins forgiven, and God's Word gives us the answer by making us *"wise unto salvation."*

The Bible goes on to say, *"All scripture is given by inspiration of God, and is profitable for doctrine..."* *"Doctrine"* is what we believe and teach. We find in the Bible what we are to believe about everything–about life and death, heaven and hell, angels, things to come, immorality, decency, and such issues as homosexuality.

Our philosophy for life should come out of the right theology, our knowledge of God and His Word.

The Bible is also given to us *"...for reproof..."* This means to point out to us where we are wrong. No one likes to hear he is wrong, but the Bible is the truth and truth reveals error. There is no telling how far we could drift if we did not have the Bible to reprove us.

Our philosophy for life should come out of the right theology, our knowledge of God and His Word.

The Bible says God's Word is also given to us to correct us. This means to show us what is right.

Then the Word of God says, *"...for instruction in righteousness...."* The Holy Spirit applies the Bible to our lives. He patiently stays with us until we are doing what is right.

"That the man of God may be perfect..." In this context, the Lord is not speaking only of a preacher, but of every Christian. The word *"perfect"* means "complete." Everything we need to complete our lives is given to us in Scripture. Remember our thoughts concerning the necessity of all Scripture. Do not run first to some book on your shelf. Of course, many books are helpful. I have written many that I hope are helpful. But go first *to* God's Word and do not go *from* God's Word. The books we read should only point us to God's Word.

"...throughly furnished unto all good works." In the Bible, we find everything we need to equip us to be the laborers we must be. Look no further than God's Word for a manual for Christian service.

We should say, "God, I'm ashamed of how little I know of Thy Word. I'm ashamed of how little of Thy Word I read. I'm ashamed of how little of Thy Word I've memorized. I'm ashamed of how little of Thy Word I'm able to meditate on because I know so little of it. Lord, I'm going to spend more time with Thee in Thy Word."

We should say, "Lord, I'm ashamed of how little of Thy Word I've acted upon and how many times I've heard what I should do and never obeyed." Obedience is not doing God's will; it is delighting in doing God's will.

Hudson Taylor was a wonderful missionary to China. He was an inspiration to untold thousands, giving himself to God and the Chinese people. Taylor had a son, Howard, who married a fine Christian lady. She knew when she married Howard Taylor that he was going to serve the Lord. She said, "We'll go anywhere but China." God led them to China.

In the Bible, we find everything we need to equip us to be the laborers we must be.

As they stood on the deck of the ship, about to leave for China, other missionaries gathered with them. Standing on the deck of the ship she thought, "Here I am, surrounded by missionaries, and I am disobedient to God. I do not want to go to China. This one thing is keeping me from having God's peace." She was not delighting in God's will.

As she stood on the deck of that ship, she heard a sailor call out to the captain, "All is clear, Captain! All is clear, Captain! Full steam ahead!"

As she heard that sailor call to the captain, "All is clear!" God convicted her and she looked up to heaven and said, "All is clear, Christ! All is clear, my Lord Jesus! Full steam ahead to China!"

We are given God's Word that we might "observe to do according to all that is written therein."

I want to say to God at this moment, "All is clear, dear Lord! All is clear. Whatever, whenever, wherever, all is clear! All is clear!" Can you say to God, "All is clear"?

God has given us His Word. Joshua 1:8 declares, *"This book of the law shall not depart out of thy mouth; but thou shalt meditate therein day and night, that thou mayest observe to do according to all that is written therein."* We are given God's Word that we might *"observe to do according to all that is written therein."* As you read your Bible, heed what God says. Look to the Lord and declare that "all is clear" and that you are willing to do whatever He commands you to do.

TRUTHS TO REMEMBER

The Bible is the eternal Word of God (Psalm 119:89).

The Bible is God's fixed point of reference in a world that is always changing (II Timothy 3:13-17).

Every word of the Bible and all the Bible is inspired, or "God-breathed" (II Timothy 3:16; Matthew 4:4).

The Bible is a true record because it is God-breathed and God cannot lie (Psalm 119:151).

It is impossible to be spiritual without being scriptural (I Corinthians 2:13).

Every Christian should read the Scriptures, search the Scriptures, meditate on the Scriptures, and memorize the Scriptures (Psalm 119:11, 97; John 5:39).

When attempting to speak the truth, it is always best to use the very language of the Bible (II Timothy 1:13).

In every book of the Bible, God has a specific message for His children (II Timothy 3:16).

We need to know all sixty-six books of the Bible because each book helps us to be the children God desires for us to be (II Timothy 3:16-17; Matthew 4:4).

Jesus Christ is our all-sufficient Savior. We are complete in Him because He is everything we need (Colossians 2:9-10).

God's Word is all-sufficient. Everything we need to complete our lives is given to us in Scripture (II Timothy 3:16-17).

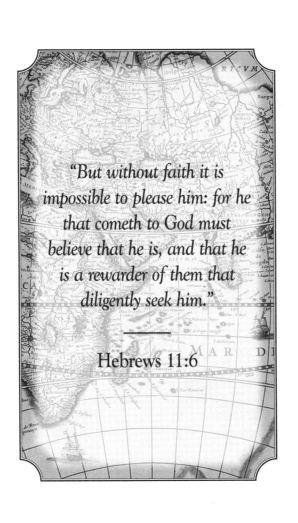

"But without faith it is impossible to please him: for he that cometh to God must believe that he is, and that he is a rewarder of them that diligently seek him."

——

Hebrews 11:6

CHAPTER THREE

GOD HEARS AND ANSWERS PRAYER

G od hears and answers the prayers of His children. To be a child of God, we must realize that we are separated from God because of our sin. The payment of our sin debt is death and hell.

The Lord Jesus Christ was born of a virgin and sent forth by God into this world. He became a man without ceasing to be God. He lived a sinless life. Though He owed no sin debt, He went to the cross, and the sins of the whole world were laid upon Him. He tasted death for every man. He died and was buried in a borrowed tomb. On the third day, He came forth from the grave, alive forevermore.

When we ask Him to forgive our sin and we trust His finished work on the cross for our salvation, He hears and answers our prayer. He forgives our sin and comes to live in our lives forever.

At that moment, we are born into God's family. This is a spiritual birth. We become children of God. Each child of God has the privilege of talking regularly, through prayer, to his heavenly Father.

God's Word tells us in Hebrews 11:6, *"But without faith it is impossible to please him: for he that cometh to God must believe that he is, and that he is a rewarder of them that diligently seek him."*

God hears and answers prayer. We must believe that God is and believe that He rewards them that diligently seek Him. God extends an invitation to His children in Jeremiah 33:3, inviting them to come unto Him and to call upon Him. *"Call unto me, and I will answer thee, and shew thee great and mighty things, which thou knowest not."*

When considering the subject of prayer, all of us feel like failures. Though we pray, it seems we know so little about praying. In Ephesians chapter three, speaking of what God can do, the Bible gives us an amazing promise. The Bible says in Ephesians 3:20-21,

> *Now unto him that is able to do exceeding abundantly above all that we ask or think, according to the power that worketh in us, unto him be glory in the church by Christ Jesus throughout all ages, world without end. Amen.*

Dr. John R. Rice wrote a wonderful book about prayer explaining that prayer is simply asking and the answer to prayer is receiving. This may seem oversimplified for some people, but I must admit that Dr. Rice knew more about praying than I know.

One of the greatest mistakes we make in the Christian life is getting the idea that increased activity will make us more spiritual. We get so involved in things and become so busy with things that we forget the important thing. The important thing should be talking with God and allowing Him to speak to us, calling unto God and allowing Him to hear and answer our prayers. God hears and answers prayer.

To get started the right way in the matter of prayer, we must first admit our failure to pray. In the Gospel according to Luke, the disciples came with inquiring hearts to the Lord Jesus. In Luke 11:1 the Bible says, *"And it came to pass, that, as he was praying in a certain place, when he ceased, one of his disciples said unto him, Lord, teach us to pray, as John also taught his disciples."*

We instruct people by what we say. We inspire people to action by what we do.

We instruct people by what we say. We inspire people to action by what we do. When the disciples saw the Lord Jesus praying, they knew it was the custom of His life to pray. They wanted Him to teach them how to pray. He was the greatest Teacher who ever lived, yet they did not say, "Lord, teach us to teach." He was the greatest Preacher who ever lived, yet they did not say, "Lord, teach us to preach." They said, "We want to be able to talk to God; teach us to pray." It was not a matter of teaching them "how" to pray. It was a matter of being motivated to pray.

Some people have the idea that if we study prayer we become more effective in prayer. Beholding a painting does not make one an artist. It may create a desire to become an artist, but a person does not become an artist unless he puts a brush in his hand and starts to paint.

Studying the subject of prayer will not necessarily make us more effective in prayer. We trust that it creates an interest and a desire to pray; but studying the subject, without being moved to action, will not make us more effective in prayer.

There are many prayers that go unanswered. Some people say God answers every prayer, either yes or no. What I mean by unanswered prayer is that God will not hear it and He says no. There are many prayers that go unanswered because there are conditions God gives in answering prayer.

How many times have we heard someone pray, "Lord, open the windows of heaven and pour out a blessing"? In the last book of the Old Testament, the book of Malachi, the Bible says in chapter three, verses eight through ten,

> *Will a man rob God? Yet ye have robbed me. But ye say, Wherein have we robbed thee? In tithes and offerings. Ye are cursed with a curse: for ye have robbed me, even this whole nation. Bring ye all the tithes into the storehouse, that there may be meat in mine house, and prove me now herewith, saith the LORD of hosts, if I will not open you the windows of heaven, and pour you out a blessing, that there shall not be room enough to receive it.*

The condition to God's opening the windows of heaven is that we are faithful in the matter of giving and paying the tithe to the Lord. Blessings are attached to a condition; unless we meet the condition, God will not pour out the blessing. If there are things we want from God, we need to know there are conditions to God's providing those answers to prayer.

God tells us why He will not answer certain prayers. The Bible says in Matthew 6:5, *"And when thou prayest, thou shalt not be as the hypocrites are: for they love to pray standing in the synagogues and in the corners of the streets, that they may be seen of men. Verily I say unto you, They have their reward."*

God says that if we pray just to be seen of men or if we pray just for people to hear our words, He will not hear our prayers. Occasionally, people pray as if they are trying to teach God something. They pray, "Lord, you remember when..." or "Lord, you know..." God already knows everything; we do not need to attempt to teach Him anything. What they are really doing is speaking to the audience. We are all somewhat guilty of this.

The Bible says in verse seven of the same chapter, *"But when ye pray, use not vain repetitions, as the heathen do: for they think that they shall be heard for their much speaking."* In certain parts of the world, especially those so heavily steeped in false religions, there are habitual times of prayer that include prayers which resemble chants; they relate very well to this verse of Scripture.

If there are things we want from God, we need to know there are conditions to God's providing those answers to prayer.

Sometimes when we pray, especially around mealtime, our prayers are no more than vain repetitions. We should thank God for the food He has provided and ask Him to sanctify it, but often we get in such a hurry that we do not take time to pray. We run in and, as a ritual, repeat something as a child would repeat it. Something can be said quickly from your heart, but God will not hear vain repetitions.

We should ask why we want things from God. In James 4:3 the Bible says, *"Ye ask, and receive not, because ye ask amiss, that ye may consume it upon your lusts."*

Many times, we want our prayers answered for ourselves and not for the Lord and His glory. We might as well be praying in our name and not His name. Most of us who have lived into adulthood can look at our lives in retrospect and thank God that He did not hear some of our prayers. If we had received everything we had asked for, we would be in bad shape. God will not hear prayers that are asked for our own lusts.

Stay in an attitude of prayer as you face the decisions that confront you during the day.

The two things for which God holds me most accountable are the two hardest things for me to do: to spend time with God in His Word and to pray.

You might safely say that the minister should read the Bible and pray more than others read the Bible and pray. If it is something the pastor should do, it is something we all should do. We cannot separate prayer from our Christian lives; prayer should be at the very heart of our lives.

Let us pray each evening, thanking God for His care and keeping of our lives through the day and seeking His aid for our sleep during the night. As we awake from sleep, let us pray and acknowledge that the day belongs to God. Pray before each meal. Stay in an attitude of prayer as you face the decisions that confront you during the day. Pray with those in need. God's Word says in I Thessalonians 5:17-18, *"Pray without ceasing.*

In every thing give thanks: for this is the will of God in Christ Jesus concerning you."

Though we profess to know the Lord Jesus as our Savior, we really have no Christian life without the Bible and prayer; we only exist. It is easy to know the things to say, to turn the automatic button on without really having our hearts touched.

There are people who have been effective in prayer, whose lives are exemplary in the matter of prayer. One such person was George Mueller. He came to the place in his life when all that mattered to him was to live his life in a way that was approved unto God. For ten years, he got out of bed every morning and the first thing he did was pray. Sometimes he would pray for fifteen minutes; sometimes he would pray for half an hour; sometimes he would pray for an hour. He was like Robert Murray McCheyne who said, "I will see no man's face until I see the face of God."

For ten years Mueller began his day this way. He got out of bed and immediately got on his knees and prayed. Then he realized he was going about it the wrong way. He said he should have brought his life in tune with God first, doing what

Robert Murray McCheyne said, "I will see no man's face until I see the face of God."

was necessary to be happy in the Lord as a Christian. He used the passage in Ephesians chapter six, not just to prove his point–his point had already been proven in practice–but to prove it for those he was trying to help. The Bible says in Ephesians 6:17-18,

> *And take the helmet of salvation, and the sword of the Spirit, which is the word of God:*

praying always with all prayer and supplication in the Spirit, and watching thereunto with all perseverance and supplication for all saints.

He began taking the time to read God's Word first and to bring his heart in tune with the Lord. He made his heart happy in Jesus Christ, then entered into His presence through prayer.

The Bible reveals God to us. Prayer brings God's power to us. The point Mueller made is absolutely correct. When we try to pray, our old nature says, "Don't pray, you don't need to pray. You can make it on your own. You can work it out." Our old nature says, "You don't need God, you can do it yourself."

When we do take the time to read God's Word and feed our souls, letting God speak to us through His Word, we find happiness in Christ; we are brought in tune with the Lord. We can speak to Him as we would speak to a friend.

PRAY BECAUSE THE DEVIL IS REAL

Why should we pray? We should pray because the Devil is real. We are not going to win the victory against Satan without prayer. The Bible says in Ephesians 6:10-12,

Finally, my brethren, be strong in the Lord, and in the power of his might. Put on the whole armour of God, that ye may be able to stand against the wiles of the devil. For we wrestle not against flesh and blood, but against principalities, against powers, against the rulers of the darkness of this world, against spiritual wickedness in high places.

In the Word of God, we learn we can defeat the Devil through prayer. We must pray because the Devil is real. When we do not pray, we leave the door open for the Devil to enter. He, *"as a roaring lion, walketh about, seeking whom he may devour."* He will walk by our door a thousand times to find it open once. All Satan is looking for is the moment of his greatest temptation and the moment of our greatest weakness to come together.

> *All Satan is looking for is the moment of his greatest temptation and the moment of our greatest weakness to come together.*

Man does not sin without will; therefore, he must be strengthened to exercise his will against the Devil. When our Lord Jesus taught His disciples, He said, *"Lead us not into temptation, but deliver us from evil"* (Matthew 6:13). Temptation is not sin; yielding to temptation is sin. We should ask the Lord to keep us from temptation. There are places I should not go; there are things I should not look upon or listen to. There are some things that should not enter my eye gate or ear gate because Satan will use my weaknesses.

All of us are studied by Satan and his demons, especially those of us who are trying to serve God and do His will. We should depend upon God as helpless babies because the Devil is real. We need to depend upon the Lord.

The Word of God says in Ephesians 6:12, *"For we wrestle not against flesh and blood, but against principalities, against powers, against the rulers of the darkness of this world, against spiritual wickedness in high places."*

PRAY TO CONFESS YOUR SINS

The Bible says in I John 1:9, *"If we confess our sins, he is faithful and just to forgive us our sins, and to cleanse us from all unrighteousness."* To *"confess"* our sins means to say the same thing about them that God says. As God's children, we should not harbor unconfessed sins in our lives. We need to keep short accounts with God. Go to God in prayer every day to confess your sins and find forgiveness and cleansing in Him.

PRAY TO RECEIVE THINGS FROM GOD

We should pray because this is the way God has designed for us to receive things from Him. The Bible says in James 4:2, *"Ye lust, and have not: ye kill, and desire to have, and cannot obtain: ye fight and war, yet ye have not, because ye ask not."*

There is a God in heaven who has everything we need. He says the way to get things from Him is through prayer. God can do all things. He owns all things. He can provide all things. God has made a way to get things from Him and that is through prayer.

PRAY TO DEAL WITH WORRIES AND CARES

We should pray because prayer will eliminate our worries and cares. The Bible says in Philippians 4:5-7,

> *Let your moderation be known unto all men. The Lord is at hand. Be careful for nothing; but in every thing by prayer and supplication with*

thanksgiving let your requests be made known unto God. And the peace of God, which passeth all understanding, shall keep your hearts and minds through Christ Jesus.

This is a precious promise. We should pray because our worries and cares can be done away with through prayer. We are so anxious about things, and most of the things we get anxious about never come to pass. We live such worrisome lives. The reason for this is not our personalities or our upbringing. The reason we live such anxious lives is our prayerlessness. We should pray because this is the only way to deal with our worries and cares.

PRAY FOR GOD TO MEET YOUR NEEDS

We should pray because God meets our needs through prayer. Hebrews 4:15-16 says,

For we have not an high priest which cannot be touched with the feeling of our infirmities; but was in all points tempted like as we are, yet without sin. Let us therefore come boldly unto the throne of grace, that we may obtain mercy, and find grace to help in time of need.

Perhaps at this moment you are in a time of great need. In time of need, we should come before the Lord. He has made a way to meet our needs.

There are two things we are constantly dealing with all our lives. One is lust. Every one of us has lust in his heart. We all have lust, the desire to have, the desire to do, the desire to be.

All of us must deal with the lust of the flesh, the lust of the eyes, and the pride of life.

We must also deal with lure. The world and the Devil make sure something is always dangling in front of us. People say, "I never had such a hard time until I decided I was going to live for God." When we make a decision to give our lives to Christ, the Devil does everything in his power to destroy us. The Devil gets much credit that he does not deserve; the world is out there luring us also.

In time of need, we can go to the throne of grace. Praying is God's way of meeting our needs.

PRAY IN THE NAME OF THE LORD JESUS CHRIST

We should pray because God has invited us to pray in Jesus' name. Why should we pray in the name of the Lord Jesus Christ? There is no name like Jesus' name. His name is the name of power and authority. There are awful moments of temptation when we simply cry out in Jesus' name, "Jesus, help me!" To pray in Jesus' name means to pray for His sake and for His glory. The Bible says in John 14:1-6,

> *Let not your heart be troubled: ye believe in God, believe also in me. In my Father's house are many mansions: if it were not so, I would have told you. I go to prepare a place for you. And if I go and prepare a place for you, I will come again, and receive you unto myself; that where I am, there ye may be also. And whither I go ye know, and the way ye know. Thomas saith*

*unto him, Lord, we know not whither thou goest;
and how can we know the way? Jesus saith unto
him, I am the way, the truth, and the life: no man
cometh unto the Father, but by me.*

Have you ever been in a place where you needed directions, and you asked someone, "Can you tell me how to get to...?" The person gave you the directions and you followed the directions. You may have been in the same situation and asked someone, "How do you get to...?" and he answered, "Let me show you." The difference is that one person told you the way and the other person became the way.

The Lord Jesus did not say, "Let Me tell you the way." He said, *"I am the way."* He is the way. When we come into His presence, He is the way. He wants us to pray in His name.

The Bible says in John 14:13, *"And whatsoever ye shall ask in my name, that will I do, that the Father may be glorified in the Son."*

> *When we pray, we would do well to learn to pray in the name of the "Lord Jesus Christ." This is His full title, and it speaks of His authority and power.*

If we ask anything in His name, He will do it. This is powerful. When we pray, we would do well to learn to pray in the name of the *"Lord Jesus Christ."* This is His full title, and it speaks of His authority and power. We should pray because He has invited us to pray in His name, the name of all power and authority. In John 16:23-26 the Bible says,

*And in that day ye shall ask me nothing.
Verily, verily, I say unto you, Whatsoever ye shall*

ask the Father in my name, he will give it you.
Hitherto have ye asked nothing in my name: ask
and ye shall receive, that your joy may be full...
At that day ye shall ask in my name: and I say
not unto you, that I will pray the Father for you.

We should pray because He has invited us to come in His name, seeking what we need.

PRAY BECAUSE JESUS CHRIST IS PRAYING FOR YOU

We should pray to the God who hears and answers prayer because the great work of Jesus Christ at this moment is the work of intercession. The Lord Jesus Christ's earthly ministry was the great work of redemption. On Calvary, He bled and died, was buried in a borrowed tomb, and He came forth from the grave, alive forevermore. The great work of Christ, at this moment, is the work of interceding. He is interceding for us. Has He heard from you lately?

In the book of Hebrews, we see the great Interceder. Hebrews 7:25 says, *"Wherefore he is able also to save them to the uttermost that come unto God by him, seeing he ever liveth to make intercession for them."*

He, Jesus Christ, ever liveth to make intercession for us. In I Timothy 2:5 the Bible says, *"For there is one God, and one mediator between God and men, the man Christ Jesus."*

We should pray because Christ is seated at the right hand of the Father ever living to make intercession for us.

We pray or we fail. We pray or we worry ourselves sick. We pray or we live defeated lives. We pray or we dishonor God. We pray or we struggle through life, drifting aimlessly. We pray or the Devil is the victor. There is no middle ground.

Years ago, when I was a very young Christian, a man who is now in heaven, Dr. Vance Havner, said in my presence, "As long as you can take it or leave it, you'll leave it."

May God work in our lives until we get to the place where there are no options, only prayer. Something might happen with your marriage or with one of your children. You may lose your job or your health. God works in the lives of His children to the point where we have no options. We can only pray. If we see things the way God sees them, there are no options. The only way to have victory is to pray in faith. God hears and answers prayer.

TRUTHS TO REMEMBER

God hears and answers the prayers of His children (Jeremiah 33:3; Hebrews 11:6).

Through prayer, every child of God has the privilege of talking regularly with his heavenly Father (Luke 11:2-4; Hebrews 4:15-16).

Our prayers will not be answered if we do not meet the conditions set forth in God's Word (John 15:7; Malachi 3:8-10).

God will not hear our prayers if we pray to be seen of men (Matthew 6:5).

We are not to use vain repetitions when we pray (Matthew 6:7).

God will not hear prayers that are asked for our own lusts (James 4:3).

Every Christian should take time each day to read God's Word and to enter into His presence through prayer. It is good to pray at the beginning and ending of each day and to pray before meals (Psalm 5:3; Psalm 55:17; I Timothy 4:5).

Through prayer we can defeat the Devil (Ephesians 6:10-18).

We should pray to confess our sins to God (I John 1:9).

Prayer is the way God has designed for us to receive things from Him (James 4:2).

We can deal with worries and cares through prayer
(Philippians 4:5-7).

God will meet our needs as we seek Him in prayer
(Hebrews 4:15-16).

We are to pray in the name of the Lord Jesus Christ
(John 14:13; 16:23-26).

We should pray because Jesus Christ is seated at the right
hand of the Father, ever living to make intercession for us
(Hebrews 7:25).

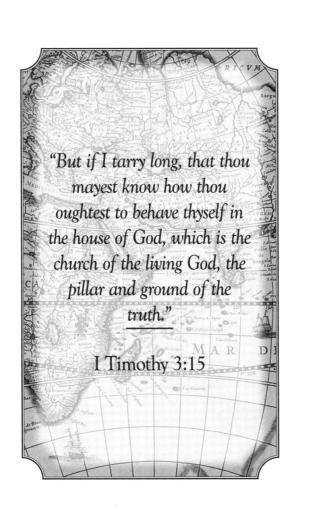

"But if I tarry long, that thou mayest know how thou oughtest to behave thyself in the house of God, which is the church of the living God, the pillar and ground of the truth."

I Timothy 3:15

CHAPTER FOUR

WHAT THE BIBLE TEACHES ABOUT THE NEW TESTAMENT CHURCH

I t is our responsibility to rightly divide God's Word as we deal with what the Bible says about the Jew, the Gentile, and the church. What we believe about the church must come from the Bible. The Bible is our sole authority for faith and practice in the New Testament church.

Our philosophy must come out of our theology. What we believe as Christians must come from what we know about God. In other words, it is disastrous to develop a philosophy for life without building that philosophy on the right theological foundation.

The Lord Jesus said, *"I will build my church."* The word translated *"church"* is very significant because it is never used to describe a denomination. It is never used to describe a group of churches. It is never used to describe a national church. The Bible teaches that every church is to be directly accountable to God, not to a denomination or group of churches.

When someone asks, "What is the church?" I give a very simple definition. The local church is a group of baptized believers who have voluntarily joined themselves together to carry out the Great Commission. This is about as simply as one can state it.

> *The local church is a group of baptized believers who have voluntarily joined themselves together to carry out the Great Commission.*

In Matthew 16:13, the Lord Jesus asked His disciples when He came to the coast of Caesarea Philippi, *"Whom do men say that I the Son of man am?"*

They started answering, *"Some say that thou art John the Baptist."*

No doubt when the people heard Him thundering forth the Word of God with such mighty authority they said, "This has to be none other than John the Baptist."

They said, "Some say Elijah." When they saw the miracles of the Lord Jesus, they thought, "This is a prophet of miracles. This must be Elijah." But He was not Elijah.

They said, "Some say Jeremiah." No doubt when the people saw the tears of Jesus Christ, our weeping Savior, they thought of the tender compassion and tears of the prophet Jeremiah.

Then the Lord Jesus asked His disciples in verse fifteen, *"But whom say ye that I am?"*

Simon Peter stepped forward and said, *"Thou art the Christ, the Son of the living God."*

The Lord Jesus took that statement and said in verse eighteen, *"Upon this rock I will build my church; and the gates of hell shall not prevail against it."* His church is His called-out assembly. As we read this statement, we can place the emphasis in any number of places. Let us emphasize *"I will."* The Lord will get it done. The church has many enemies and critics, but Jesus Christ is everlastingly at it. He is building His church.

It is important for us to note that the Lord Jesus said, *"I will build my church."*

He did not say, "I will build *your* church." He did not say, "*You* will build my church." He said, *"I will build my church."* Those who seek to market the church and practice target evangelism want to tell us that it is our business to be church builders. No, God gives the increase. He builds the church. We have one responsibility–to be obedient to the Lord. As we obey the Lord, the Lord will build His church. All I need to know is what God wants me to do.

> *He did not say, "I will build* your *church." He did not say, "*You will *build my church."* He said, "I will build my church."

We need to teach our people that the Lord is doing His work in this world through the local church. The pastor of a New Testament church needs to help people see how they can serve the Lord by finding their place in the local church.

The Lord Jesus said, *"I will build my church."*

THE NEW TESTAMENT CHURCH STARTED WITH CHRIST AND HIS DISCIPLES AND WAS EMPOWERED AT PENTECOST

People need to know simple things about the local church. The church started with Christ and His disciples and was empowered at Pentecost. This is vital.

When I was in seminary, I was given the assignment of writing a rather long paper about when the church started. In my research, I discovered more than a dozen different ideas concerning when the church began.

From my own study of God's Word, I have come to the conviction that the church started with Christ and His disciples and was empowered at Pentecost. When we come to this conclusion, we realize that the Lord gave the Great Commission to the church, not simply to a group of believers. The ordinances of the church, baptism and the Lord's Supper, are not ministerial ordinances; they are local church ordinances.

Of course, the emphasis of the New Testament is on the local church. Consider what we find in Matthew chapter eighteen. When the Lord Jesus speaks again of the church in verses fifteen through seventeen, He says,

> *Moreover if thy brother shall trespass against thee, go and tell him his fault between thee and him alone: if he shall hear thee, thou hast gained thy brother. But if he will not hear thee, then take with thee one or two more, that in the mouth of two or three witnesses every word may be established. And if he shall neglect to hear them, tell it unto the church: but if he neglect to hear*

*the church, let him be unto thee as a heathen
man and a publican.*

The so-called "invisible church" would have a hard time
hearing this matter. The Lord said, *"my church."* This is an
organized group that the Lord said one could speak to, and
when necessary, exercise church discipline within.

THE NEW TESTAMENT CHURCH HAS A SAVED MEMBERSHIP

The next thing that Christians should know about the New
Testament church is that the church has a saved membership. In
Acts 2:41-42 the Bible says,

*Then they that gladly received his word were
baptized: and the same day there were added unto
them about three thousand souls. And they
continued stedfastly in the apostles' doctrine and
fellowship, and in breaking of bread, and in prayers.*

Here we read of those who believed on Jesus Christ and
obeyed the Lord in baptism. When you ask a man if he is saved,
he may tell you that he is saved but does not belong to a local
church. But the local church, as we find it in God's Word is
made up of a saved membership, people who have been saved
and obeyed the Lord in believer's baptism.

From the example we find in the Bible, we learn that people
"joined" the local body of believers. Acts 9:26 speaks of Paul
"joining" himself to the church. Not only should we be
Christians, we should be obedient to Christ in believer's baptism
and belong to a local, Bible-believing, Bible-preaching church.
Each one of us should put his life and influence with other

believers who have voluntarily joined themselves together to carry out the Great Commission. As God gives us health and strength, we should faithfully attend the services of the church and support the work of the Lord through the local church with our prayers, finances, and labors of love.

From this passage, we learn that those who were added to the church were saved and followed the Lord in baptism. Also, there was a body of doctrine connected with this church. They continued steadfastly in the apostle's doctrine.

In order for baptism to be biblically correct, there must first be the right authority, which is the local church. The Lord gave this authority to the local church.

The Lord Jesus said in Matthew 28:19-20,

> *Go ye therefore, and teach all nations, baptizing them in the name of the Father, and of the Son, and of the Holy Ghost: teaching them to observe all things whatsoever I have commanded you.*

When Christ gave the command for believers to be baptized, He spoke to the local church.

Second, there must be the right mode of baptism, which is immersion. Immersion is going in the water, under the water, and up out of the water. This is not sprinkling water on people. Immersion is the only mode of baptism that pictures our death with the Lord Jesus Christ, our burial with the Lord Jesus Christ, and the new life we have in Christ.

Third, there must be the right candidate for baptism. This is a saved person. People must be saved before they follow the Lord in baptism.

THE NEW TESTAMENT CHURCH HAS CHRIST AS THE ONLY HEAD

Another thing we need to know about the local church is that Christ is the only head of the church.

The Bible says in Colossians 1:18, *"And he is the head of the body, the church: who is the beginning, the firstborn from the dead; that in all things he might have the preeminence."*

An independent Baptist church recognizes that it only has one headquarters, and that is heaven. The church has only one head, and that is the Lord Jesus.

The body of doctrine that the Lord Jesus gave to His disciples when He established the church is the same body of doctrine that we Baptists hold dear today. We trace our roots to the Lord Jesus and His disciples knowing that, throughout the centuries, God has always had a people who believed the same body of doctrine that Christ gave to His disciples.

> *The body of doctrine that the Lord Jesus gave to His disciples when He established the church is the same body of doctrine that we Baptists hold dear today.*

We have a Book, the completed revelation of God, the Bible, and winding through the centuries, people have had the same body of doctrine to hand to the next generation.

The word *Baptists* can be remembered by an acrostic which is often used concerning the distinctives of our Baptist faith.

"B" stands for *biblical authority*. The Bible is the sole authority for our faith and practice. We do not find out what we are and go to the Bible to try to find out if we can justify what we are doing and what we are. We go to the Bible to find out what we are supposed to be and try to conform to the image that we have found in God's Word.

"A" stands for the *autonomy of the local church*. We believe that every church we find in the New Testament was a self-governing church, with only Christ as the head.

"P" represents the *priesthood of believers*. Every believer has access to God through Jesus Christ.

"T" stands for the *two church officers*–pastors and deacons. We find these officers in the New Testament.

"I" stands for *individual soul liberty*. Most people, when they are asked, say that the sole authority of the Scripture in our faith and practice is the single most important distinctive of our faith. However, in actuality, you will find that growing out of individual soul liberty, we find every other distinctive. If we did not have individual soul liberty, we could not come to the convictions we have come to on all these other matters.

"S" stands for a *saved church membership*.

"T" represents *two church ordinances*–baptism and the Lord's Supper. These are the things that Jesus Christ ordered that we do. Both of these things are pictures of His sacrifice for us on the cross of Calvary.

"S" stands for *separation of church and state*. Of course, some people have reinterpreted this expression in our times to be something entirely different than what our founding fathers meant for it to mean in our country.

These are what we call distinctives of Baptist people. Baptist distinctives are often given in this acrostic form so they are easier to remember.

Our faith was once delivered, but it must be contended for in every generation. The Bible says in Jude 3,

> *Beloved, when I gave all diligence to write unto you of the common salvation, it was needful for me to write unto you, and exhort you that ye should earnestly contend for the faith which was once delivered unto the saints.*

Some think that Jude took pen in hand and had a desire to write about the common salvation, but God directed him differently. This is exactly opposite of what this passage teaches.

The writer, the human penman God used, declared, "Because I am writing to you of the common salvation, it is needful for me to write unto you to earnestly contend for the faith." We lose the message unless we contend for the faith. We are going to answer to the Lord Jesus for this matter of contending for the faith.

Nothing is to take the place of Jesus Christ as head of the church.

Nothing is to take the place of Jesus Christ as head of the church. This will take care of the idea of denominationalism. There may be someone who would say that being "independent" is not a safe position, that we need some sort of denominational hierarchy or headquarters to keep us in line. Since when would human instrumentality be safer than Jesus Christ and His holy Word? The Lord Jesus is the only head of the New Testament church.

THE NEW TESTAMENT CHURCH IS THE PILLAR AND GROUND OF THE TRUTH

The Bible teaches us that the church is *"the pillar and ground of the truth."* The Bible says in I Timothy 3:15-16,

> *But if I tarry long, that thou mayest know how thou oughtest to behave thyself in the house of God, which is the church of the living God, the pillar and ground of the truth. And without controversy great is the mystery of godliness: God was manifest in the flesh, justified in the Spirit, seen of angels, preached unto the Gentiles, believed on in the world, received up into glory.*

Often people assign some responsibility to the church that is not a biblical assignment. Using the very words of Scripture, the church is *"the pillar and ground of the truth."*

I like the imagery God uses when He says, *"The pillar and ground of the truth."* We are taking the truth to people in every generation. Think what a staggering responsibility we have in our churches to be the pillar and ground of the truth.

In our world, we have traded truth for tolerance. Millions refuse to have any fixed point of reference. A local church is the pillar and ground of the truth.

In our world, there is no lack of knowledge, but there is a great lack of truth. We live in an information age, and we are bombarded, overloaded, and absolutely overwhelmed with knowledge; but it is truth we need. We must lift up the truth in love.

THE NEW TESTAMENT CHURCH IS AN INDEPENDENT CONGREGATION

The church we find in the New Testament is an independent congregation. In Acts thirteen, the great church in Antioch was about to send out missionaries. The Bible says in Acts 13:1-4,

> *Now there were in the church that was at Antioch certain prophets and teachers; as Barnabas, and Simeon that was called Niger, and Lucius of Cyrene, and Manaen, which had been brought up with Herod the tetrarch, and Saul. As they ministered to the Lord, and fasted, the Holy Ghost said, Separate me Barnabas and Saul for the work whereunto I have called them. And when they had fasted and prayed, and laid their hands on them, they sent them away. So they, being sent forth by the Holy Ghost, departed unto Seleucia; and from thence they sailed to Cyprus.*

The people of the church sent them out, but the Word of God also says the Holy Ghost sent them out. Which is it? Were they sent by the Holy Ghost or sent by the church?

They were sent by both. The church recognized the Spirit of God at work. This local congregation acted independently of any other congregation. As we read about the church in the Bible, we are reading about local, independent congregations. Each congregation was autonomous and indigenous, meaning that they were self-governing and self-supporting.

One of the great errors being made in independent Baptist churches today is that people talk about how much they are like every other church in town. We need to point out the distinctives of the New Testament church and show people that our churches are entirely biblical in their distinctives.

THE NEW TESTAMENT CHURCH IS RESPONSIBLE TO EVANGELIZE THE WORLD

In Acts 1:8 the Bible says,

> *But ye shall receive power, after that the Holy Ghost is come upon you: and ye shall be witnesses unto me both in Jerusalem, and in all Judaea, and in Samaria, and unto the uttermost part of the earth.*

What can one church do in a world of six billion people? We need to see our place in God's work to evangelize the world.

> *There is a world of difference between* ambition *and* vision. *Ambition is something that comes from men. Vision is something that comes from God.*

Just imagine if every local, independent congregation felt the consuming burden given by the Lord to go into all the world and preach the gospel to every creature.

Churches have lost their vision. There is a world of difference between *ambition* and *vision*. Ambition is something that comes from men. An ambitious man cannot be helped. He is interested only in doing more to magnify the flesh. Vision is something that comes from God. It is God who has vision. Our vision is simply doing what God has already stated clearly in His Word that needs to be done.

The vision God gives us is always a world vision. If you find a New Testament church, you will find a local church that has taken seriously God's command for world evangelism.

It is the responsibility of each local church to start other churches. May God grant us a mighty revival of church planting and send New Testament church pioneers into His harvest field.

THE NEW TESTAMENT CHURCH IS PASTOR-LED

Sheep need a shepherd, and our Lord has designed that the local church be led by a shepherd–their pastor.

This man is not a hireling; he is a shepherd. He loves the sheep and gives his life for the sheep.

I Timothy 3:1 says, *"This is a true saying, If a man desire the office of a bishop, he desireth a good work."* The word *"bishop"* is a word God uses synonymously with *elder* and *shepherd*. These are different terms for the same office. *"Bishop"* means "one who can see and oversee." The man of God should be a man who sees farther than others in the church because God gives him discernment. He is a discerning man who recognizes things earlier than perhaps others recognize them. When little devils pop up, he is going to fight the little devils because he discerns that there is going to be a big devil someday if he does not fight the little ones.

There are battles to be fought. These are tests God brings to prove the pastor. The pastor leads the people as he looks to the Lord.

God enables the pastor. Just as God raised up Joshua in the eyes of the people, the Lord will prove Himself through the pastor to the people of the church as the pastor seeks wisdom from God to deal with the problems. They will recognize that they have God's man to lead them.

Do not run from your problems; run to the Lord. God said to Moses, *"Go down to Egypt and tell Pharaoh to let my people go."* If anyone knew about Pharaoh, Moses did. I have a suspicion that Moses thought he would have been much better off if God would have killed Pharaoh and said, "Moses, he's dead so you can lead the people out." God does not kill our Pharaohs. He goes with us to meet them.

Every New Testament church should be a pastor-led church.

Every New Testament church should be a pastor-led church. There are people you are going to meet in your church who cannot lead and will not follow. This is a tough crowd to handle. But if the pastor will get in the saddle and ride, God will ride with him. If he says, "Here we go, people! The Lord Jesus is leading us forward," the church will follow. The New Testament church is a pastor-led church.

God's Word gives us the clear pattern for the New Testament church. Jesus Christ said, *"I will build my church."* Our responsibility is to follow Christ and be obedient to Him. May the Lord help each one of us to find our place of service in the local New Testament church.

TRUTHS TO REMEMBER

The Bible is our sole authority for faith and practice in the New Testament church (I Timothy 3:14-15).

Our philosophy for life must come out of our theology. What we believe as Christians must come from what we know about God (Colossians 2:8; I Corinthians 3:11; Colossians 1:16-18).

The local church is a group of baptized believers who have voluntarily joined themselves together to carry out the Great Commission (Acts 2:41-42).

Jesus Christ builds the church as we are obedient to Him (Matthew 16:18).

The church started with Christ and His disciples and was empowered at Pentecost (Matthew 16:13-18, 18:15-18; Acts 1:8).

The Lord Jesus gave the Great Commission to the church, not simply to a group of believers (Matthew 28:18-20; Mark 16:15; Luke 24:46-48; John 20:21; Acts 1:8).

The ordinances of the church, baptism and the Lord's Supper, are not ministerial ordinances; they are local church ordinances (Matthew 28:19; I Corinthians 11:23-34).

The New Testament church is made up of members who have been saved and baptized (Acts 2:41-42).

Every believer should join a local New Testament church and place his life and influence with that body of believers (Acts 9:26; Acts 2:41,47).

Scriptural baptism requires the right authority, the local church; the right candidate, a saved person; and the right mode, immersion (Matthew 28:19-20; Acts 2:41; Mark 1:9-11; Acts 8:35-39).

The Lord Jesus Christ is the only head of the New Testament church (Colossians 1:18).

The body of doctrine that the Lord Jesus gave to His disciples when He established the church is the same body of doctrine that we Baptists hold today (Acts 2:42).

The New Testament church is the pillar and ground of the truth. We must lift up the truth in love (I Timothy 3:15; Ephesians 4:15).

The New Testament church is an independent congregation (Acts 13:1-4).

The New Testament church is responsible to evangelize the world. It is the responsibility of each local church to start other churches (Acts 1:8).

The New Testament church is a pastor-led church (I Timothy 3:1-7).

Every believer should find his place of service in a local New Testament church and should faithfully attend that church (Acts 2:41-47; Hebrews 10:25).

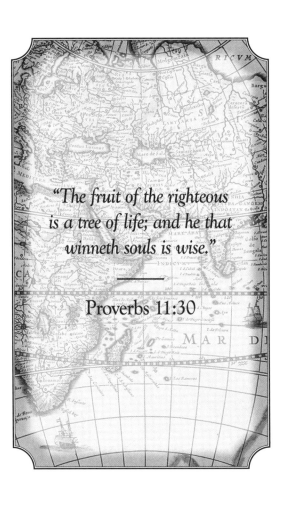

"The fruit of the righteous
is a tree of life; and he that
winneth souls is wise."

———

Proverbs 11:30

CHAPTER FIVE

HE THAT WINNETH SOULS IS WISE

I t is the responsibility and privilege of every Christian to be a soul winner. The Bible says in Proverbs 11:30, *"The fruit of the righteous is a tree of life; and he that winneth souls is wise."* It has been nearly two thousand years since our Lord left the church with the sacred responsibility of giving the gospel message to the world. So few who say they are His followers have obeyed Him. Let us take a fresh look at what He has charged us to do.

THE COMMAND OF CHRIST

Our highest motive in the matter of soul winning must be one of love for our Savior, and out of this love comes a desire to obey His command. As we read the Scriptures, we find that Christ's command has been very clearly given.

> *Go ye therefore, and teach all nations, baptizing them in the name of the Father, and of the Son, and of the Holy Ghost: teaching them to observe all things whatsoever I have commanded you: and, lo, I am with you alway, even unto the end of the world. Amen* (Matthew 28:19-20).

> *And he said unto them, Go ye into all the world, and preach the gospel to every creature* (Mark 16:15).

> *And said unto them, Thus it is written, and thus it behoved Christ to suffer, and to rise from the dead the third day: and that repentance and remission of sins should be preached in his name among all nations, beginning at Jerusalem. And ye are witnesses of these things* (Luke 24:46-48).

> *Then said Jesus to them again, Peace be unto you: as my Father hath sent me, even so send I you* (John 20:21).

> *But ye shall receive power, after that the Holy Ghost is come upon you: and ye shall be witnesses unto me both in Jerusalem, and in all Judaea, and in Samaria, and unto the uttermost part of the earth* (Acts 1:8).

So often the highest motive for personal evangelism is mentioned as being the need of mankind; but according to the Word of God, our highest motive should be the love of Christ. Paul said, *"For the love of Christ constraineth us"* (II Corinthians 5:14). Christ was motivated by obedience to the Father and love to go to Calvary, and it should be the love of

Christ that motivates us to witness to others. Paul was compelled to go after souls because of the love of Christ.

At times, the sinfulness of men keeps us from loving them as we should. If our motive for evangelism is our love for lost men, that motive will not be strong enough. The love of Christ is the only motive that will drive us to face great disappointment, defeat, or danger. When our motive for evangelism is the love of Christ, we will not resign our task when rejected by sinners.

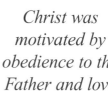

Christ was motivated by obedience to the Father and love to go to Calvary, and it should be the love of Christ that motivates us to witness to others.

The Lord Jesus prepared His disciples to win the lost by using the right motivation. He said, *"He that hath my commandments, and keepeth them, he it is that loveth me"* (John 14:21). The Lord Jesus knew the strength of love. Love begets love. Christ loved His disciples and, on the basis of their love for Him, He charged them with the vital responsibility of world evangelism. Our obedience to His command is the real proof of our love for Him. The Bible basis for soul winning is love. The Word of God clearly states, *"For this is the love of God, that we keep his commandments"* (I John 5:3).

THE CONDITION OF THE UNSAVED

Dr. Jonas Salk devoted much of his life to the discovery of a vaccine to cure polio. His life's efforts were rewarded by the discovery of the vaccine. Imagine for a moment, that after Dr. Salk's discovery of the vaccine, he had withheld it from all those who needed it. Unthinkable? Yes, but there are multitudes of Christians with lost and dying humanity at their doorstep, and they never make any effort to tell them of the Savior.

The tragic symptoms of sin sickness call us to the matter of soul winning. There are many symptoms. A few that most of us recognize are listed below.

EMPTINESS

Men without Christ are empty. A life cannot be complete without Christ. The Bible says, *"But as many as received him, to them gave he power to become the sons of God, even to them that believe on his name"* (John 1:12). It is only when men receive Christ that the emptiness of their lives is filled.

WITHOUT MEANING

Multitudes could be called "aimless wanderers." The lost man has no purpose or direction. He may find temporary meaning in a material goal, but the deepest longings of his heart will not find satisfaction without Christ. The Lord Jesus said, *"I am the way."* His way is the only way to find meaning in this life.

FEAR OF DEATH

To the unsaved, death is a frightening journey into the unknown. To the Christian, it is the door that opens into an eternity with the Lord Jesus. He has promised to give us grace and strength to overcome this great fear. He said, *"I am the resurrection, and the life: he that believeth in me, though he were dead, yet shall he live: And whosoever liveth and believeth in me shall never die"* (John 11:25-26).

LACK OF INNER PEACE

The lost man has no peace in his soul. The Lord Jesus is the only One who can bring this peace. He said to His disciples after He had announced to them that He was to be crucified, *"Peace I leave with you, my peace I give unto you: not as the world giveth, give I unto you. Let not your heart be troubled, neither let it be afraid"* (John 14:27).

Christ takes care of more than the symptoms. He is the cure for the disease.

LONELINESS

There is no friend like the Lord Jesus. Hebrews 13:5 gives us the promise, *"I will never leave thee, nor forsake thee."* The unsaved man does not have a constant companion who will never leave or forsake him.

The sin disease reflects itself in many symptoms in our society. Christ takes care of more than the symptoms. He is the cure for the disease. The Bible is very plain in declaring the condition of those without Christ.

LOST

"For the Son of man is come to seek and to save that which was lost" (Luke 19:10).

PERISHING

"For God so loved the world, that he gave his only begotten Son, that whosoever believeth in him should not perish, but have everlasting life" (John 3:16).

UNDER GOD'S WRATH

"He that believeth on the Son hath everlasting life: and he that believeth not the Son shall not see life; but the wrath of God abideth on him" (John 3:36).

CONDEMNED ALREADY

"He that believeth on him is not condemned: but he that believeth not is condemned already, because he hath not believed in the name of the only begotten Son of God" (John 3:18).

WITHOUT HOPE

"That at that time ye were without Christ, being aliens from the commonwealth of Israel, and strangers from the covenants of promise, having no hope, and without God in the world" (Ephesians 2:12).

BLINDED BY THE DEVIL

"But if our gospel be hid, it is hid to them that are lost: in whom the god of this world hath blinded the minds of them which believe not, lest the light of the glorious gospel of Christ, who is the image of God, should shine unto them" (II Corinthians 4:3-4).

ON THE ROAD TO HELL

"Enter ye in at the strait gate: for wide is the gate, and broad is the way, that leadeth to destruction, and many there be which go in thereat" (Matthew 7:13).

DEAD ALREADY IN SIN

"And you hath he quickened, who were dead in trespasses and sins" (Ephesians 2:1).

THE SIN OF SILENCE

Because we know the Lord Jesus as our personal Savior, we are indebted to tell the unsaved of Him. To have means to owe. The apostle Paul wrote to the church at Rome in Romans 1:14-16,

> *I am debtor both to the Greeks, and to the Barbarians; both to the wise, and to the unwise. So, as much as in me is, I am ready to preach the gospel to you that are at Rome also. For I am not ashamed of the gospel of Christ: for it is the power of God unto salvation to every one that believeth; to the Jew first, and also to the Greek.*

> Because we know the Lord Jesus as our personal Savior, we are indebted to tell the unsaved of Him.

The world owes us nothing, but we owe the world the message of salvation.

There is a powerful story in the book of II Kings, chapter seven, that illustrates the sin of silence. Beginning with verse three, the story tells of four lepers who sat at the entrance of the city gate. Their city, Samaria, was under siege by the Syrian army. People inside the city were dying of hunger. These lepers decided to leave their place at the gate of the city and enter the camp of the enemy. To their glad surprise, the Syrian army had been frightened away by the Lord, and the lepers found everything they needed.

It is sinful and ugly to do nothing, when it is in our power to do good.

Suddenly, they remembered the starving masses back in the city and they said one to another, *"We do not well: this day is a day of good tidings, and we hold our peace: if we tarry till the morning light, some mischief will come upon us: now therefore come, that we may go and tell the king's household"* (II Kings 7:9). They returned to the city and told the good news. Likewise, our day is a day of much tragedy, but we have found the Good News. That Good News is Christ.

It is a terrible sin to be silent when we have the Good News that the world needs to hear. It is sinful and ugly to do nothing, when it is in our power to do good. The Bible says, *"Therefore to him that knoweth to do good, and doeth it not, to him it is sin"* (James 4:17).

The only way to start soul winning is to start! Many excuses have been offered by men for not attempting to win the lost. These excuses will not stand when we face God. Most every excuse offered will fall into one of the following categories:

"IT IS NOT MY RESPONSIBILITY."

It has already been clearly stated that soul winning is every Christian's job. The Lord has placed this matter of highest importance in our hands. He has chosen men to tell the gospel story. Only the ransomed can tell the story of the soul set free. As Christians, if we do not tell others how to be saved, the simple yet profound truth is that they will never hear! It is our responsibility.

"MEN WILL NOT LISTEN."

While it is true that there is a great deal of indifference among the lost, many will listen. Many are waiting to hear the Good News. Some speak of their fear of offending those who do not want to hear, when the real problem is not our fear of offending others; it is our fear of others offending us. Remember, we have a story to tell even if they will not listen.

Our heavenly Father loves us so much that He would not charge us with a responsibility without providing for us the necessary power for the task.

We have been given divine authority to tell others of the Savior. We have a God-given right to *"go into all the world and preach the gospel to every creature."* We need not wait for an invitation. We have already been commanded to go. Our Lord knows the need of mankind, and He has called us to speak to that need. Men realize that there is something missing in their lives, even though they do not recognize what that missing element is. It is our responsibility as Christians to show them that it is Christ they need.

"I AM NOT ABLE."

Perhaps in no other area do so many of us feel weak, yet our God has commanded us to go. Our heavenly Father loves us so much that He would not charge us with a responsibility without providing for us the necessary power for the task.

Our strength comes from the indwelling Holy Spirit. He gives us power and makes us able. He speaks through us as we yield to Him. He gives us the wisdom we so desperately need. Our fear of failure can be used to thrust us to total dependence on the Holy Spirit for soul-winning enablement. Christ said, *"Follow me, and I will make you fishers of men"* (Matthew 4:19).

Our purpose is to win souls. Our program is to seek out the lost. Our position is that of an ambassador for Christ. Our proclamation is the gospel. Our power is the Holy Spirit. Be a Christian who seeks to win souls.

TRUTHS TO REMEMBER

Jesus Christ clearly commanded that we are to take the gospel message to every creature (Matthew 28:19-20; Mark 16:15; Luke 24:46-48; John 20:21; Acts 1:8).

The love of Christ is our highest motivation for witnessing to others (II Corinthians 5:14).

Without Christ people are empty, without purpose or direction, fearful of death, without inner peace, and lonely. This should stir our hearts to tell them of Jesus Christ (Matthew 9:36; John 14:27; Psalm 40:2-3).

The Bible teaches that people without Christ are "dead in trespasses and sins" and are "condemned already." They must hear the gospel and believe on the Lord Jesus Christ in order to be saved (Ephesians 2:1; John 3:18).

Because we know Jesus Christ as our personal Savior, we are indebted to tell the unsaved of Him. To be silent is sin (Romans 1:14-16; James 4:17).

God would not charge us with this responsibility without providing for us the necessary power for the task. We are enabled by the indwelling Holy Spirit to be a witness for Christ (Acts 1:8; Matthew 28:20).

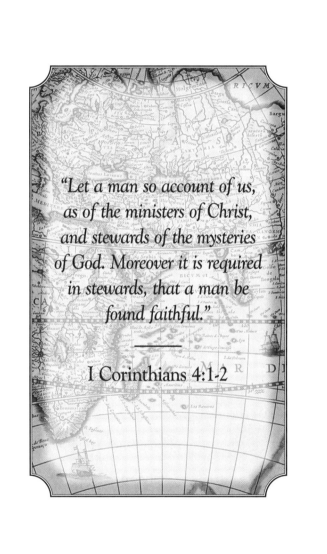

"Let a man so account of us,
as of the ministers of Christ,
and stewards of the mysteries
of God. Moreover it is required
in stewards, that a man be
found faithful."

———

I Corinthians 4:1-2

CHAPTER SIX

GIVING IS THE GOLDEN KEY TO GOD'S BLESSING

DR. TOM SEXTON

P eople who believe the Bible is God's Word believe that it is the final authority in life. I Corinthians 6:19 says, *"What? know ye not that your body is the temple of the Holy Ghost which is in you, which ye have of God, and ye are not your own?"*

In verse nineteen the word *"What?"* is read as a shocking word. *"What?"* Did you ever hear someone tell you something that shocked you so much that you said, "What? Say that again!" In I Corinthians 6:19, the word "What?" comes out of shock and dismay. *"What? know ye not that your body is the temple of the Holy Ghost which is in you, which ye have of God, and ye are not your own? For ye are bought with a price: therefore glorify God in your body, and in your spirit, which are God's"* (I Corinthians 6:19-20).

If you are a Christian, the Bible says you are not your own. You are bought with a price. As Christians, we belong to the Lord Jesus Christ.

We have been redeemed by His blood. He owns everything that we have. It is all His. We are simply stewards of what He has given us. The Bible says in I Corinthians 4:2, *"Moreover it is required in stewards, that a man be found faithful."*

Psalm 50:10 says, *"For every beast of the forest is mine, and the cattle upon a thousand hills."* The Lord said the cattle on a thousand hills, literally every beast, belongs to Him. Not only do they belong to the Lord, but also the hills on which the cattle are standing belong to God.

The Bible says in Haggai 2:8, *"The silver is mine, and the gold is mine, saith the LORD of hosts."* All the silver and all the gold belong to the Lord. It is all His. You may say, "I have a gold mine." No, you are borrowing that gold mine. It belongs to the Lord. God said that all the silver and all the gold and all the precious stones belong to Him.

> *We have been redeemed; we have been bought with a price. The price was Christ's precious blood.*

Psalm 24:1 says, *"The earth is the LORD's, and the fulness thereof; the world, and they that dwell therein."* Not only does God say that He owns the cattle on a thousand hills and the hills on which the cattle stand; not only does God say that He owns the silver and gold and all the precious stones; but God also says, *"The earth is the LORD's, and the fulness thereof; the world, and they that dwell therein."* In other words, God owns everyone and everything.

We have been redeemed; we have been bought with a price. The Bible says in I Corinthians 6:20, *"Ye are bought with a price."* The price was Christ's precious blood. He shed His blood for you and for me.

I want you to think about being a good steward. We should be good stewards in these three areas: tithing, giving, and faith promise giving.

TITHING

We should be good stewards in our tithing. Let us make sure we understand what the Bible has to say about stewardship. You have a choice just as I do. You can choose to believe what the Bible says, or you can choose not to believe. I believe the Bible.

When I got saved, I made a decision to trust what the Bible says. The preacher told me that God loved me and that the Lord Jesus died for me. He said that I owed a debt, and that, because Jesus Christ paid it in full, I could be saved. That night I did what the Bible says to do.

Many times in my life I have had to make decisions based solely on what the Bible teaches. When the Bible teaches something different from what I think and what I believe, I do what the Bible says to do.

Malachi 3:8-12 says,

> *Will a man rob God? Yet ye have robbed me. But ye say, Wherein have we robbed thee? In tithes and offerings. Ye are cursed with a curse: for ye have robbed me, even this whole nation.*

> *Bring ye all the tithes into the storehouse, that there may be meat in mine house, and prove me now herewith, saith the LORD of hosts, if I will not open you the windows of heaven, and pour you out a blessing, that there shall not be room enough to receive it. And I will rebuke the devourer for your sakes, and he shall not destroy the fruits of your ground; neither shall your vine cast her fruit before the time in the field, saith the LORD of hosts. And all nations shall call you blessed: for ye shall be a delightsome land, saith the LORD of hosts.*

God does not own ten percent; God owns everything. When we talk about tithing, we are talking about what God wants us to do as good stewards.

WE ARE TO BRING THE TITHE INTO THE STOREHOUSE

We are to bring the tithe into the storehouse. God's Word says in Malachi 3:10, *"Bring ye all the tithes into the storehouse."* The church is the storehouse. The Bible says in I Corinthians 16:2, *"Upon the first day of the week let every one of you lay by him in store, as God hath prospered him."*

Sunday is *"the first day of the week."* The world has convinced people that Monday is the first day of the week, but the Bible teaches that Sunday is the first day of the week.

The Bible says on the first day of the week, which is Sunday, they went to the tomb, and the angel said, *"He is not here: for he is risen, as he said"* (Matthew 28:6). The Lord Jesus rose from the grave on the first day of the week, which is Sunday, proving that He was Lord *over* the Sabbath and Lord *of* the Sabbath. He was also demonstrating that Sunday is the Lord's Day. This is why we have church on Sunday, not on Saturday.

The Bible says in I Corinthians 16:2, *"Upon the first day of the week let every one of you lay by him in store, as God hath prospered him."* Sunday is the day we should tithe to the church, which is God's storehouse.

THE TITHE IS 10%

The tithe is ten percent. The Bible says in Leviticus 27:32, *"The tenth shall be holy unto the LORD"* It is holy because it belongs to the Lord. The Bible says, *"For thou art an holy people unto the LORD thy God"* (Deuteronomy 7:6, 14:2, 21). You may say, "I don't feel as if I am holy. I don't act as if I am holy." That is why the Bible says in I Peter 1:16, *"Be ye holy; for I am holy."* God says that we should be holy and maintain a testimony for the Lord.

GOD DOES THREE THINGS FOR US WHEN WE TITHE

God does three things for us when we tithe. He prospers us by opening the windows of heaven. He promises to rebuke the devourer, and He protects the fruit of our lives.

❖ God Promises to Prosper Us by Opening the Windows of Heaven

God says in Malachi 3:10,

> *Bring ye all the tithes into the storehouse, that there may be meat in mine house, and prove me now herewith, saith the Lord of hosts, if I will not open you the windows of heaven, and pour you out a blessing, that there shall not be room enough to receive it.*

I do not know all the blessings that God has in store for us in our lifetimes, but God has a wonderful storehouse filled with the goodness and blessings of God. The Bible says in I Corinthians 2:9, *"But as it is written, Eye hath not seen, nor ear heard, neither have entered into the heart of man, the things which God hath prepared for them that love him."*

How do we receive the blessings of God on our lives? We receive God's blessings simply by bringing the tithe into the storehouse.

❖ God Promises to Rebuke the Devourer

God says if you will bring the tithe into the storehouse, He will rebuke the devourer.

Not only should we tithe because God promises to prosper us, but we should also bring the tithe because God promises to rebuke the devourer. The Lord says in Malachi 3:11, *"I will rebuke the devourer for your sakes."*

God says if you will bring the tithe into the storehouse, He will rebuke the devourer. The devourer is the one who wants to destroy God's people. I Peter 5:8 says, *"Be sober, be vigilant; because your adversary the devil, as a roaring lion, walketh about, seeking whom he may devour."*

Devour means "to make disappear." There are many people who disappear. I do not mean they disappear off the face of the earth, I mean they disappear out of churches. They are no longer teaching Sunday School, working on a bus route, or singing in the choir. They have disappeared. Many people disappear out of homes. There are many marriages from which one of the mates has disappeared. There are many children who disappear.

You may ask, "What causes that?" The Bible says the Devil is a devourer of God's people; he causes them to disappear. God's Word says that if you will bring the tithe into the storehouse, He will rebuke the devourer. The Devil will not devour you. I would bring the tithe into the storehouse if for no other reason than to get God to rebuke the Devil.

❖ God Promises to Protect the Fruit of Our Lives

God also promises that, when we tithe, He will protect our fruit. The most precious fruit we have is our families. I want God to protect my fruit. I have the power, and so do you as a Christian, to assure that the windows of heaven are open for the blessings of God on my life. I have the power as a Christian to have God intervene on my behalf and rebuke the devourer. I have the power as a Christian to have God protect my fruit. This is all done when I do what God says and bring the tithe into the storehouse.

Some people ask, "Is tithing for this age? Isn't that an Old Testament saying?" In the Old Testament, God says, "Thou shalt not kill." Are you glad we still practice that? We like pulling Old Testament things out that we like, but we do not like some of them. Let me answer this question, "Is tithing for this age?"

First of all, tithing was practiced before the Law, before God gave the Law. Tithing was practiced in Genesis 14:20 when

Abraham gave a tithe to Melchizedek. Melchizedek is a type of Christ. The Bible says, *"And he gave him tithes of all."*

Tithing was taught and practiced under the Law. Leviticus 27:30 says, *"And all the tithe...is the LORD's: it is holy unto the LORD."*

Tithing was confirmed by the Lord Jesus. If for no other reason, you should tithe because the Lord Jesus said in Matthew 23:23, *"Ye pay tithe of mint and anise and cummin, ...these ought ye to have done."*

Everything we have belongs to God. As stewards, we have to decide whether we are going to honor God with what is His.

The second question people often ask is this: "Should I tithe if I cannot afford to?" This is a good question. We have to realize something. One hundred percent belongs to God. It is not ten percent God's and ninety percent ours. Everything we have belongs to God. As stewards, we have to decide whether we are going to honor God with what is His.

I like to look at it this way. Tithing is not bringing a tenth to the Lord. Tithing is bringing God the tenth, and He gives me ninety percent. That is why it is said that the tithe should be the first check written. Proverbs 3:9 says, *"Honour the LORD with thy substance, and with the firstfruits of all thine increase."* Of course, *"firstfruits"* means what comes first.

Think about this. Most people wait until the end and say, "Well, let's see now. I have the car payment and the boat payment and my little fund and my retirement plan going, and I don't have but a couple of dollars left. I don't think I can pay God this week." They have it all turned around.

Do not let the Devil reverse it on you. Tithing is not paying God ten percent. Tithing is when God gives you ninety percent. In other words, it all belongs to God, but ninety percent is not yours until first you give God what He wants.

I Corinthians 3:9 says, *"For we are labourers together with God."* God is our partner. Can you imagine that God is in partnership with us? He owns everything. He owns the cattle on a thousand hills. He owns the gold and the silver. He owns everyone. Yet God says, "I will form a partnership with you, and I will be good to you. I will pay you ninety percent, and I will keep only ten percent."

God says, "I am going to keep ten percent." But we say, "Wait a minute. One hundred percent is mine, and I will take what I need first, and then give what is left to God." God says it this way in Malachi 3:8, *"Will a man rob God?"* The truth is, we are not honest with God until we first give God the ten percent that belongs to Him.

You may say, "I am not sure I can figure out ten percent." Then make it twenty percent to be safe. Go ahead and tithe thirty percent and make the Devil really angry! You cannot out-give God.

I met a man once who said, "Preacher, one day I decided I was going to tithe by faith, too." I said, "I have never heard of faith-tithing."

He said, "I know what I make, but I am going to start tithing on what I want to make. By faith I am going to start." So he started tithing on what he wanted to make.

He said, "Do you know what I found out? God made sure that He was not in debt to me. The more I tithed, the more God increased my income." God will not be in debt to anyone.

God does not want anyone robbing Him, and God says bring the tithe. The tithe is the first ten percent, not the last ten percent. When we give God the ten percent that belongs to Him, God gives us the ninety percent that is left. What a Savior He is to do something like that!

Can you imagine your boss coming up to you and saying, "Now, listen. We made $10,000 this week. Here it is." You say to the boss, "Okay, here is $1,000 for you." He says, "All right. Here is $9,000 for you."

The next week you go in, and he says, "We made $10,000 again." You say, "Now this week I need $9,999." He says, "I am sorry. Now you get nothing. You give me my ten percent first, and I will give you what is left. If you think you are going to take what you want and give me what is left, we are not doing business anymore." You would be wise to give him what he wants first.

You may say, "I cannot afford to tithe." No, you cannot afford *not* to tithe. The child of God should not be considering the question of whether or not he can afford to tithe. He should ask himself if he wants to live the life of a thief or honor the Lord.

Here is another question people ask: "Should I give my tithe to the local church?" Yes, the local church is the storehouse. *"Bring ye all the tithes into the storehouse."* People say, "I believe in the 'universal' church." They do not know what they are saying. See if that "universal" pastor will help them!

Acts 1:8 says, *"And ye shall be witnesses unto me both in Jerusalem."* First of all, we must reach Jerusalem. Then we need to reach Judaea and Samaria, and then the uttermost part of the earth. But we must start in our Jerusalem.

How do you reach your Jerusalem? Do you call the preachers on television? Do you send them your tithe? Call them when you have problems! You will find out they will pick up the phone and try to find a local church! A local church is going to help you.

Once a man said to me, "My former pastor told me if I didn't agree with the church, I didn't have to give them my tithe."

I said, "Really? That's interesting. What did he say to do with it?"

This man replied, "He said I should put it in a coffee can. Then when I can find something I can agree with, I can give it to that ministry."

I prayed, "Lord, give me something that this man will understand." God gave me this as I was talking to him.

I said, "The Lord Jesus is our example. Do you believe that?"

He said, "Yes, I do."

I said, "He is our example. As a matter of fact, He is every Christian's example. If we have any questions about what we should do, we should do what the Lord Jesus did. We should follow His example. I Peter 2:21-22 says, *'Ye should follow his steps: who did no sin, neither was guile found in his mouth.'*

You may say, "I cannot afford to tithe." No, you cannot afford not to tithe.

"Do you think the Lord Jesus worked? He was known as the carpenter's son. He was a carpenter. Do you think He worked?" He said, "Oh, yes, there is no doubt about it. He worked." I said, "When He worked, He got paid. He was a working man. As a working man, He made some money. What do you think He did with that money? Did He tithe?

"Well, He must have tithed because in John 8:46 He asked the Pharisees and scribes and all those religious people who tried to find fault with Him, *'Which of you convinceth me of sin?'* If they could have put their finger on one thing, they could have proven He was not Christ.

> *Tithing is not giving; it is bringing. When we tithe, we are bringing to the Lord what already belongs to Him.*

"He also made this statement that no one else has ever made. He said in Matthew 5:17 that He came to fulfill the Law. Sitting in that crowd among His critics was one rabbi who knew Him, because he was the rabbi in the synagogue that He attended. If the Lord Jesus was a God-robber, if Jesus did not tithe, that rabbi would have stood up and said, 'I bring accusation against Him. I have known Him for thirty years. I have never known Him to bring the tithe into the storehouse.'

"The fact that no one was able to accuse the Lord Jesus of disobeying God's Word is proof that He was a tither. Did the Lord Jesus agree with everything that went on in the synagogue? No. Yet He still brought the tithe. Even if a person disagrees with some practice in his local church, that is not grounds for disobeying the Lord's command."

Tithing is not giving; it is bringing. When we tithe, we are bringing to the Lord what already belongs to Him.

Some people say, "I am giving my tithe." No, it is not your tithe to start with. How in the world can you give it? It is God's tithe. You do not give someone something that is his already; you bring it back to him. The tithe belongs to God. You do not give it. I do not give it. We bring it. When we do not bring it, we are robbing God. God commands us in His Word, *"Bring ye all the tithes."*

By the way, do not ask anyone to try to figure this out. Do not sit down with pencil and paper and figure out if you can afford to tithe. You will come up every time with the answer "no."

When I got saved, I owed much more than my income, especially after I started earning a living the honest way. My income was drastically cut after I got saved. I thought, "What in the world am I going to do? Maybe I can just work hard and get my debts paid and then I can tithe." I asked my preacher, "What should I do?" My pastor said, "Do not rob God. Tithe." So I said, "Okay." By faith my wife and I brought the tithe into the storehouse.

Do not sit down with pencil and paper and figure out if you can afford to tithe. You will come up every time with the answer "no."

When I went to Bible college, we had a tremendous amount of expense on our home, and I did not make enough money to pay all the bills, but by faith we tithed. There were Mondays that we started off with nothing but pocket change, and sometimes we did not even have pocket change, but I am here to say that God has met every need that we have ever had.

God has opened the windows of heaven and blessed us. God has been good to us. We did not sit down and figure out whether we could tithe. We just went ahead and did what we should, and God took care of us.

You say, "I want to be a good steward." Are you a tither? Are you bringing the tithe to the Lord?

GIVING

We should be good stewards in giving. Giving does not come from the ten percent. Giving should come from the ninety percent that you have left. You may say, "I do not have much left out of the ninety percent after I pay my bills." Then start working to try to get something. Figure out what you can do sacrificially.

> *Give, and it shall be given unto you...For with the same measure that ye mete withal it shall be measured to you again.*

The Bible says in Luke 6:38,

Give, and it shall be given unto you; good measure, pressed down, and shaken together, and running over, shall men give into your bosom. For with the same measure that ye mete withal it shall be measured to you again.

The Bible does not say "Bring" in this verse; the Bible says *"Give."* You do not *give* the tithe; you *bring* the tithe. But the remaining ninety percent is yours, and God says to give out of that. If you give, God will bless your life. Giving is not tithing. Tithing is not giving.

A pastor friend of mine was telling me about his first job. He was a teenager and made twenty dollars. His Christian mother sat down with him and asked, "What belongs to God?" My friend said that he took two dollars and put it aside.

Then she asked, "What are you going to give the Lord?" He said, "Here is my offering, these two dollars."

She said, "That is not yours, that is the Lord's. Your offering comes out of the eighteen dollars you have left after the tithe." The pastor told me that was one of the greatest lessons he has ever learned about giving.

Many people believe they have given when they tithe. However, our giving comes out of the ninety percent left after the tithe. Tithing is bringing the ten percent. Giving comes out of the ninety percent.

When you give, God says He will give to you. When you give, God says men shall give into your bosom.

Many faithful Christians have had promotions and wonder, "How in the world did I get a promotion?" I will tell you how. They did what God wanted them to do. They gave, and God made sure men gave to them.

Some Christians cannot explain the things that have happened. They bought a piece of property that later became very valuable. How in the world did that happen? Are they such geniuses? No. They gave, and God made sure men gave to them. This is the way it works.

Many people believe they have given when they tithe. Tithing is bringing the ten percent. Giving comes out of the ninety percent.

If you will read the book of Acts, you will find out that God's people gave. They gave sacrificially. God not only wants us to tithe, but God also wants us to give.

You cannot explain it any other way. God will bless you if you give. Whatever you do will prosper. God will make sure that people will come and give into your bosom. He will make sure that you have your needs met. If you will give, God will take care of you.

FAITH PROMISE GIVING

Faith promise giving is asking the Lord to enable us to give beyond ourselves. Faith promise giving is for Christians who have become faithful tithers and have given sacrifically out of their budget for the cause of Christ yet want to do more, beyond their power.

The Bible says in II Corinthians 8:1-5,

> *Moreover, brethren, we do you to wit of the grace of God bestowed on the churches of Macedonia; how that in a great trial of affliction the abundance of their joy and their deep poverty abounded unto the riches of their liberality. For to their power, I bear record, yea, and beyond their power they were willing of themselves; praying us with much intreaty that we would receive the gift, and take upon us the fellowship of the ministering to the saints. And this they did, not as we hoped, but first gave their own selves to the Lord, and unto us by the will of God.*

Faith promise giving is asking God to lay upon our hearts an amount that He will give to us. Faith promise giving is asking God for something, and God answers you and blesses your life. It can begin so small.

Many Christians never get to that level. They never say, "Let's pray for ten dollars. Let's pray for this. Let's pray for that."

They never get serious about it and say, "Lord, we do not have any more money. We brought the tithe. We sacrificed as much as we could sacrifice. But oh God, there is a need here, and we believe You want to meet that need. If You would let us by faith have a part in it, help us, dear Lord. Meet the need through us. Lord God, prove that we are Your children. Give us something so we can make a difference in the lives of people. Oh God, You own the cattle on a thousand hills. You own the gold. You own the land. You own the earth. Oh God, help us meet this need."

God wants us to live beyond our power. God does not simply call us to do what we can do in our own power. God does not simply call us to do what we can do with our own abilities and talents. God not only calls us to do the possible, He calls us to do the impossible.

> *God wants us to live beyond our power. God not only calls us to do the possible, He calls us to do the impossible.*

Oh, let us not see what we can do. Let us see what God can do. God's Word says in Luke 1:37, *"For with God nothing shall be impossible."*

Do you want to be a good steward? The Bible says in I Corinthians 4:2, *"Moreover it is required in stewards, that a man be found faithful."*

Dear friend, let God prove He is God. God wants to prove Himself. Let Him. Maybe you have been robbing God. You need to pray, "Lord, I am not going to rob You anymore. I am going to tithe."

Maybe you need to pray with your family and say, "God, help us to figure out how we can give sacrificially for Your work."

Maybe your family needs to pray, "Oh God, help us to have faith. Lord, help us to go beyond our abilities. Prove something to my family. Prove something to my children. Oh God, prove You are God. Lord, by faith, we claim it."

TRUTHS TO REMEMBER

As Christians, we belong to the Lord Jesus Christ; we have been redeemed by His precious blood (I Corinthians 6:19-20).

Everything we have belongs to Jesus Christ; we are simply stewards of what He has given us (I Corinthians 4:2; Psalm 50:10; Haggai 2:8; Psalm 24:1).

We are to bring the tithe into the storehouse, which is the local church. The tithe is ten percent (Malachi 3:10; I Corinthians 16:2; Leviticus 27:32).

When we bring the tithe, God will prosper us by opening the windows of heaven and pouring out a blessing upon us (Malachi 3:10; I Corinthians 2:9).

God promises to rebuke the devourer, the Devil, when we bring the tithe (Malachi 3:11; I Peter 5:8).

When we tithe, God will protect the fruit of our lives (Malachi 3:11).

Tithing should take first priority in our finances (Proverbs 3:9).

If we do not bring the tithe, we are robbing God (Malachi 3:8).

Tithing is not giving; it is bringing. When we tithe, we are bringing to the Lord what already belongs to Him (Malachi 3:10).

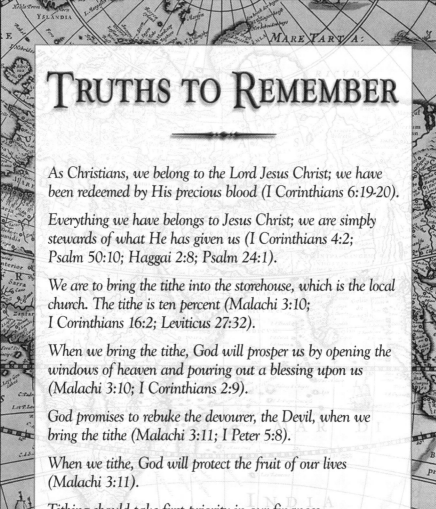

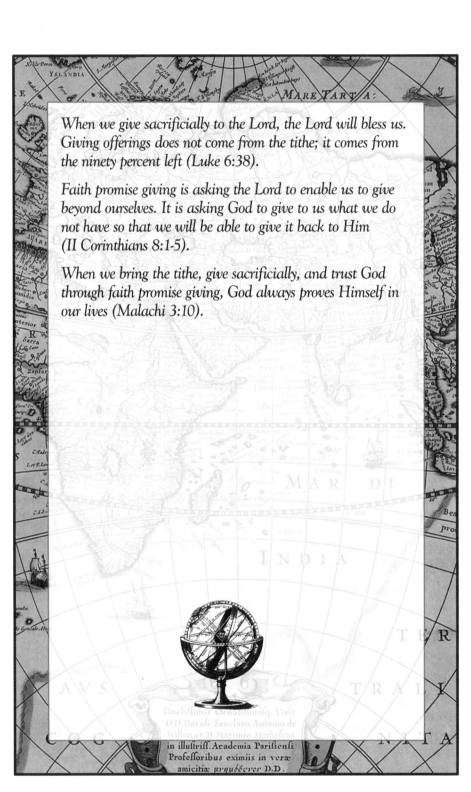

When we give sacrificially to the Lord, the Lord will bless us. Giving offerings does not come from the tithe; it comes from the ninety percent left (Luke 6:38).

Faith promise giving is asking the Lord to enable us to give beyond ourselves. It is asking God to give to us what we do not have so that we will be able to give it back to Him (II Corinthians 8:1-5).

When we bring the tithe, give sacrificially, and trust God through faith promise giving, God always proves Himself in our lives (Malachi 3:10).

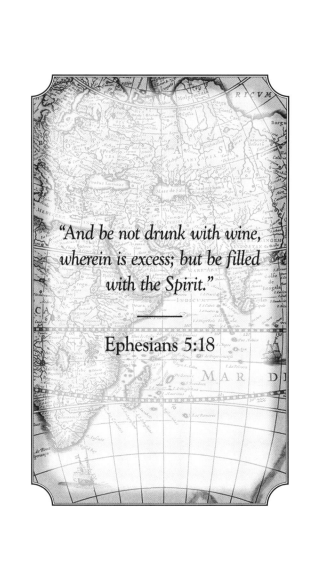

"And be not drunk with wine,
wherein is excess; but be filled
with the Spirit."

———

Ephesians 5:18

WE ARE COMMANDED TO BE FILLED WITH THE HOLY SPIRIT

Do you know the Spirit of God? Do you commune with Him? Do you fellowship with Him? The Spirit of God is co-equal, co-existent, eternally existent with God the Father and God the Son. When we speak of the Holy Spirit, we speak of God. The Bible says we are to be filled with the Spirit. Ephesians 5:18 says, *"And be not drunk with wine, wherein is excess; but be filled with the Spirit."*

This is a powerful, life-changing verse of Scripture. Everything we need to live the Christian life victoriously is wrapped up in this verse.

When we trust the Lord Jesus Christ as our Savior, we realize that we all come to Christ the same way. John 3:16 says, *"For God so loved the world, that he gave his only begotten Son, that whosoever believeth in him should not perish, but have everlasting life."*

I thank God for the day that someone explained to me that I was a lost sinner and told me that if I died in my sin, I would not go to heaven. He told me that the Lord Jesus died for me. Christ not only died for me, He bore the sins of the whole world in His own body. He was buried, and He rose from the dead. He is alive forevermore. He came forth from the grave victoriously. Christ said in Revelation 1:18, *"I am he that liveth, and was dead; and, behold, I am alive for evermore, Amen; and have the keys of hell and of death."* That day I bowed my head before the Lord and asked God to forgive my sin. By faith I received Jesus Christ as my Savior. The Bible says in John 1:12, *"But as many as received him, to them gave he power to become the sons of God, even to them that believe on his name."*

When I received Christ, the Holy Spirit, who is God, came to live in me. I received all of God that I will ever receive at the moment I was saved, but He wants more and more of me with each passing day. When I trusted Him as Savior, He came into the throne room of my life, but day by day I must allow Him to be on the throne of my life.

There is a great deal of confusion about the doctrine of the Holy Spirit. It is impossible to deal with all the doctrine of the Holy Spirit in one brief lesson, but there are some things we can come to understand. Many people are ignorant of the truth of God's Word concerning the Holy Spirit and Holy Spirit fullness. However, there is something much more tragic than ignorance. It is Christians who are not ignorant, but who are indifferent to the work of the Holy Spirit of God.

The Bible says, *"Be filled with the Spirit."* Imagine taking a sponge and putting it in a bucket of water, allowing the water to be absorbed in the sponge. Is the water in the sponge, or is the sponge in the water? The answer is both. The water is in the sponge, and the sponge is in the water. When I trusted Jesus Christ as my Savior, He came to live in me; but I was also placed in Him. By the marvelous work of the Holy Spirit, I was baptized into the body of Christ by the Spirit of God, and I became a part of the body of Christ.

The baptism of the Holy Spirit is not something that is repeated. We were baptized into the body of Christ when we were saved. If this were a repeated experience, we would have to be taken out of His body, then put back in His body. The work of the baptism of the Holy Spirit is something that takes place at the time we are saved. Christ comes to live in us. We are placed in the body of Christ. This is referred to as the baptism of the Holy Spirit. We are safe and secure in Jesus Christ, and we receive everlasting life. Everlasting life does not begin the moment we die; it begins the moment we trust Christ as Savior. We have been saved from the penalty of sin. We are hell-deserving sinners, and the penalty of our sin is death and hell. *"The wages of sin is death,"* but Jesus Christ paid our sin debt in full. He died for all our sin on the cross.

Everlasting life does not begin the moment we die; it begins the moment we trust Christ as Savior.

When we trust Christ as Savior, we trust His sin payment. We are saved from the penalty of sin. Some day we shall be saved from the very presence of sin because we will no longer be in this world, but in the world to come where there is no sin. On a daily basis, we are being saved from the power of sin. Christ appeared on Calvary to save us from the penalty of sin. He shall appear in the clouds to deliver us and save us from the presence of sin. He now appears in heaven ever interceding for us to save us from the power of sin. We say we have been justified, we are being sanctified, and we shall be glorified. It is a progressive experience. The Bible teaches that the flesh is not eradicated, or done away with completely, until we receive a new body at the redemption of the body in the coming of Christ. As long as we carry our old nature around, we are going to have trouble with it. This is exactly why we need to be filled with the Holy Spirit.

When we read and hear about people being filled with the Holy Spirit, people who have been greatly used of God, sometimes the experience they talk about seems so far-reaching that it appears unattainable to the ordinary Christian. Being filled with the Spirit of God is something we should seek on a daily basis.

THE CONTEXT OF THIS PASSAGE

The context or broader text of this passage is related to the everyday life of a family. This means that Dad cannot be the father he should be without being filled with the Holy Spirit. A Christian lady cannot be the wife God wants her to be without being filled with the Holy Spirit. A Christian child should be Spirit-filled in order to live the kind of Christian life that honors and obeys his parents.

The Bible says in Ephesians 5:18, *"And be not drunk with wine, wherein is excess; but be filled with the Spirit."* Being drunk is an experience where the body is taken over by intoxication. As strange as it sounds, we are told here about the filling of the Holy Spirit, and in the same verse told not to be drunk with wine.

This comparison is very important. The drunk is under the control of another substance. The Spirit-filled person is under the control of the Holy Spirit. Drunk people do things they would not normally do if they were not drunk–they have a boldness they would never have, they attempt things they would never attempt if they were not intoxicated. The Bible says that we are to be filled with the Holy Spirit. This will affect the way we behave. If we are Christians, Christ is living in us, but that does not mean that He fills our lives.

The Bible says in verses nineteen through twenty-five,

> *Speaking to yourselves in psalms and hymns and spiritual songs, singing and making melody in your heart to the Lord; giving thanks always for all things unto God and the Father in the name of our Lord Jesus Christ; submitting yourselves one to another in the fear of God. Wives, submit yourselves unto your own husbands, as unto the Lord. For the husband is the head of the wife, even as Christ is the head of the church: and he is the saviour of the body. Therefore as the church is subject unto Christ, so let the wives be to their own husbands in every thing. Husbands, love your wives, even as Christ also loved the church, and gave himself for it.*

Being filled with the Spirit is not simply for the pulpit; it is for all of life.

God continues talking about the family in the sixth chapter. He says,

> *Children, obey your parents in the Lord: for this is right. Honour thy father and mother; which is the first commandment with promise; that it may be well with thee, and thou mayest live long on the earth. And, ye fathers, provoke not your children to wrath: but bring them up in the nurture and admonition of the Lord.*

If you want to be the father every child deserves to have, be a Spirit-filled father. Every Christian mother should say, "I want to be a Spirit-filled mother." This is the context. Being filled with the Spirit is not simply for the pulpit; it is for all of life.

When I was a young Christian, I heard about the filling of the Holy Spirit, but I thought that was only for a certain group of Christians. The context is the home. This means the filling of the Holy Spirit is for every believer.

The Command to Be Filled

Being a Spirit-filled Christian is not an option; it is a command. We are commanded to be filled with the Spirit. To disobey this command would be like disobeying any other command in the Bible. There are certain things the Holy Spirit does for us that are positional. In Ephesians 4:30 we see an example of this. The Bible says, *"And grieve not the holy Spirit of God, whereby ye are sealed unto the day of redemption."* At the moment we are saved, we are sealed. At the moment we are saved, we receive the earnest of the Holy Spirit. At the moment we are saved, we are baptized by the Spirit of God into the body of Christ. There are a number of clear teachings about what happens in our lives the moment we trust Christ as Savior. We have no control over these things. We become a part of the body of Christ. We are sealed unto the day of redemption, and we receive the earnest of the Holy Spirit.

As I stated earlier, the Holy Spirit does everything that we need to keep us safe and secure in Jesus Christ at the moment we believe. But everything we need to live the kind of Christian life we should live has to do with the filling of the Holy Spirit, which is something that we must do in obedience to the Lord. When we are filled with the Holy Spirit, we can be guided by the Holy Spirit. When we are filled with the Holy Spirit, our prayer life becomes meaningful. I do not mean by this that we have some other kind of prayer language; I mean that we understand with a discerning spirit how we should pray. When we are filled with the Holy Spirit, God produces the fruit of the Spirit in our lives. There are nine graces in that one fruit. God gives us these nine graces in Galatians 5:22-23, *"But the fruit of the Spirit is love, joy, peace, longsuffering, gentleness, goodness, faith, meekness, temperance: against such there is no law."* The fruit of the Holy Spirit comes through Holy Spirit filling.

We are commanded to be filled with the Spirit.

There are many things that happen in a Christian's life through the enabling given by the filling of the Holy Spirit. Every Christian should desire these things that we are enabled to do to live victoriously by the filling of the Holy Spirit. It is a command.

In I Corinthians 6:19-20 the Bible says,

> *What? know ye not that your body is the temple of the Holy Ghost which is in you, which ye have of God, and ye are not your own? For ye are bought with a price: therefore glorify God in your body, and in your spirit, which are God's.*

In these verses, we see clearly that our bodies are the temple of the Holy Spirit. When we look at someone, we do not see everything God sees. The Bible teaches that we are spirit, soul, and body. God's Word says in I Thessalonians 5:23, *"And the very God of peace sanctify you wholly; and I pray God your whole spirit and soul and body be preserved blameless unto the coming of our Lord Jesus Christ."*

In our spirit we have a conscience. In our soul we have intellect, emotion, and will. In our body we have five senses. When we are saved, and the Lord lives in our lives, we can live a spiritual life by living a Spirit-filled life.

The world is divided into those who are saved and those who are lost–people who have received Jesus Christ as their Savior and people who have not. Among Christians, there are those who are carnal and those who are spiritual. There are many more carnal Christians than there are spiritual Christians. We are indwelt by the Holy Spirit. We are the temple of the Holy Spirit. We are commanded to be filled with the Holy Spirit.

In I Corinthians chapter three, we find division because of carnality. The Bible says in I Corinthians 3:1-4,

> *And I, brethren, could not speak unto you as unto spiritual, but as unto carnal, even as unto babes in Christ. I have fed you with milk, and not with meat: for hitherto ye were not able to bear*

it, neither yet now are ye able. For ye are yet carnal: for whereas there is among you envying, and strife, and divisions, are ye not carnal, and walk as men? For while one saith, I am of Paul; and another, I am of Apollos; are ye not carnal?

The interesting thing is, if you tried to get all these people together, they could agree on doctrine, but they were divided over personalities. In most churches, people can agree on the doctrine of the Bible, but carnality divides the people over lesser things. Most of us are trying to treat the symptoms when the real problem in the Christian life is that we are not filled with the Holy Spirit.

If I said that I cannot be the preacher I should be without being filled with the Holy Spirit, you would agree. If I said that I cannot have the discernment I need as a pastor without being filled with the Holy Spirit, you would agree. If I said that I could not be the soul winner I should be without being filled with the Spirit, you would agree. Over thirty times the word *"witness"* is used in the book of Acts in connection with the filling of the Holy Spirit of God. We are to be witnesses. However, if I said that I cannot be the husband to my wife, the father to my children, the grandfather to my grandchildren that I should be without being filled with the Holy Spirit, you may raise an eyebrow a bit. Nevertheless, it is true. A Christian who works in an office, answering the telephone, cannot answer the phone correctly without being Spirit-filled. As a Christian, you cannot be the boss you should be without being Spirit-filled. If you are an employee, you cannot be the employee you should be as a Christian without being filled with the Holy Spirit. God does not confine the work of the filling of the Holy Spirit to one situation. Our Lord commands us to be filled. When we are not filled with the Holy Spirit, we live carnal lives. The choice is ours. We must choose either carnality or spirituality.

The Bible says in Acts 4:31,

> *And when they had prayed, the place was shaken where they were assembled together; and they were all filled with the Holy Ghost, and they spake the word of God with boldness.*

The evidence of Spirit filling is not speaking in some strange language. The evidence of Holy Spirit filling is speaking boldly in the name of the Lord Jesus Christ.

In Acts 6:5 we see the disciples searching for deacons. The Bible says, *"And the saying pleased the whole multitude: and they chose Stephen, a man full of faith and of the Holy Ghost."*

In Acts 13, we find the great missionary, Paul, being sent out from the church in Antioch. In verse nine the Bible says, *"Then Saul, (who also is called Paul,) filled with the Holy Ghost, set his eyes on him."*

We can be saved by trusting Jesus Christ as our Savior, live our entire life and never be Spirit-filled, and still die and go to heaven. However, think what it would be like when we see Jesus Christ and He says, "I had so much more for you. Why didn't you let Me bless you and use you as I wanted to?"

Do you want to be blessed and used of God the way the Lord desires to bless and use you? As we go through stages in life, there are things we realize we need at age thirty that we do not see when we are twenty. There are things we see we need to change when we are age forty that we do not see when we are age thirty, and on it goes. The Holy Spirit walks with us all through life. He enables us to move closer and closer to Jesus

Christ and be more of what we should be with each passing day. We may be growing older without growing more mature in the Lord. Why should we want to be filled with the Holy Spirit? It is not for our glory; it is for His glory.

An old friend of mine said that, when he was just a boy growing up in a rural area, his dad had a very sharp axe. He always wanted that axe because it shined and glistened in the sunlight. It was so beautiful. When he got old enough, his father gave him the axe. However, he did not give it to him to look at. He said, "Son, it is yours to use."

We may be growing older without growing more mature in the Lord.

The Holy Spirit's filling is not something to be admired or hung up for everyone to see. The Holy Spirit's filling is an enabling to live the victorious Christian life that God wants us to live. He fills us with His Spirit to enable us to do what we should do with our lives.

THE CONDITIONS OF THE FILLING

We should take special note of these conditions. We need His filling for our lives, our homes, our families, our churches, our jobs, and more importantly, for the glory and honor of our Savior. Christ is honored and glorified most from the life of a Spirit-filled Christian. The ministry of the Holy Spirit in this world is to magnify the Lord Jesus Christ. As we are filled with the Holy Spirit, our lives magnify the Lord.

We are full of ourselves. Some of the most difficult battles fought are the battles fought in the lives of the most able people.

I have seen talented singers who were not Spirit-filled but could sing beautifully. Their songs did not travel in influence as they could have traveled had they been Spirit-filled. I have seen gifted speakers who could speak beautifully, but their words did not seem to be used of God to change lives.

Dr. Lee Roberson looked me in the eye and said, "Do you want your influence to go further than you have ever imagined it would go?" I said, "Yes, sir, I certainly do." Then he said firmly, "Be filled with the Holy Spirit."

> *The ministry of the Holy Spirit in this world is to magnify the Lord Jesus Christ.*

Dr. Roberson tells the story of walking across a camp where he was speaking in New England. A young man met him as he walked across the camp. The young man said, "You spoke on the filling of the Holy Spirit. Let me ask you a question, Dr. Roberson. Are you filled with the Holy Spirit now, at this moment?" Friend, are you filled with the Holy Spirit at this moment?

What are the conditions of the Holy Spirit's filling?

THIRST

In John 7:37-39 the Bible says,

> *In the last day, that great day of the feast, Jesus stood and cried, saying, If any man thirst, let him come unto me, and drink. He that believeth on me, as the scripture hath said, out of his belly shall flow rivers of living water. (But this spake he of the Spirit, which they that*

believe on him should receive: for the Holy Ghost was not yet given; because that Jesus was not yet glorified.)

On the day of Pentecost, the Holy Spirit came to indwell every believer forever, but He is talking here about the Holy Spirit's filling. Notice the word *"thirst."* He said, *"If any man thirst..."* We must thirst for the Lord.

One great preacher of days gone by said that the secret to the filling of the Holy Spirit is absolute and total surrender to Jesus Christ, and anything the Spirit points out in your life that needs to be given to Him, at that moment, you give it to Him.

All of us have come to the altar and said, "Lord, I surrender all." Then months later, we come again before the Lord and say, "Lord, here is another area in my life I want to surrender." It is not just a life we live; it is a warfare we fight. The battles are without and within. We are losing the fight without the aid of the Holy Spirit of God.

We say we are Christians and we know we are going to heaven. We will safely make it there, but I think many of us will be ragged and torn when we arrive instead of sailing in victoriously with the filling of the Holy Spirit. There are some people at this moment who are about to be crushed underneath a heavy load that does not need to be crushing them. They could live victoriously in spite of their circumstances if they were filled with the Holy Spirit.

How is it that we thirst after God? Most of us do not know what it is to be truly thirsty–to want nothing more than a drink. We are to seek after God with a true thirst. Jesus Christ stood and cried out with a loud voice, *"If any man thirst, let him come unto me, and drink."* This filling of the Spirit begins by thirsting.

Dr. Lee Roberson has said many times that there must be emptiness and willingness in order to be filled with the Holy Spirit. This is true. We must thirst for God. Would it be good for God to make us thirsty? Yes, but we do not want to be thirsty. Many times, God must make us thirsty for His Holy Spirit's filling.

BELIEVE

In this same passage, in verse thirty-eight, we find that the second condition is believing Him. The Bible says, *"He that believeth on me, as the scripture hath said, out of his belly shall flow rivers of living water. (But this spake he of the Spirit....)"* We believe Him. We come thirsting before the Lord and say, "Lord, I thirst to be filled with the Holy Spirit, to honor and magnify the Lord."

> *We are to seek after God with a true thirst.*

If we come and believe God for this promise to be filled with the Spirit, we will serve God with more liberty and freedom. We will know in our hearts something of the nearness of Christ that we have not known. God will give us a peace we have not had to believe that He is in control and all will be well.

ASK

The third condition has to do with asking. The Bible says in Luke 11:11-13,

> *If a son shall ask bread of any of you that is a father, will he give him a stone? or if he ask a fish, will he for a fish give him a serpent? Or if*

he shall ask an egg, will he offer him a scorpion? If ye then, being evil, know how to give good gifts unto your children: how much more shall your heavenly Father give the Holy Spirit to them that ask him?

The Holy Spirit is not a substance. He is a Person. Being filled with the Holy Spirit is not like going in for a blood transfusion and getting pumped up with new energy. He is a Person. We ask for this Person to fill us. He already has residency. We need to give Him the presidency. He is already in the throne room. We need to give Him the throne. If we want to hold onto our lives and live the way we want to live, it cannot happen; but if we hunger and thirst after Him, and believe that He wants to fill us and will fill us, and we ask Him to do it, we have His promise that He will fill us.

Being filled with the Holy Spirit is not an excuse not to work. As a matter of fact, it creates a greater desire to give your life more fully to Christ.

As a young preacher, I stood in the pulpit to preach. I was struggling, toiling, working, trying. I work harder today than I have ever worked in my life. Being filled with the Holy Spirit is not an excuse not to work. As a matter of fact, it creates a greater desire to give your life more fully to Christ. I can remember clearly standing in the pulpit to preach and knowing that there had to be more to being able to preach in the liberty of the Lord. I desired to speak with freedom and honor Christ and to have much less concern about what people thought of me. I seized upon the Lord while I was speaking, breathing to God, "God, help me. Enable me." I know the Holy Spirit filled me. I learned something then about thirsting, believing, and asking. Every day of my life I want to be filled with the Holy Spirit. It is a command. We find the context in the family. The conditions are given to us. How many of us will come to the Lord and say, "Lord, fill me"?

TRUTHS TO REMEMBER

The Holy Spirit is co-equal, co-existent, eternally existent with God the Father and God the Son (II Corinthians 13:14; Matthew 28:19; Acts 5:3-4).

When we received Jesus Christ by faith as Savior, the Holy Spirit, who is God, came to live in us forever (John 14:16-17; Romans 8:9; I John 4:13).

The baptism of the Spirit takes place at the time we are saved. Christ comes to live in us, and we are placed into the body of Christ. The baptism of the Spirit is not something that is repeated (I Corinthians 12:13).

We should seek to be filled with the Holy Spirit on a daily basis (Ephesians 5:18).

When we trust Christ as Savior, we are saved from the penalty of sin. On a daily basis, we are being saved from the power of sin. Some day, when we see Jesus Christ, we shall be saved from the very presence of sin (Romans 6:23; Romans 6:6, 14; Romans 8:18-23).

The Bible teaches that the flesh is not eradicated, or done away with completely, until we receive a new body at the redemption of the body in the coming of Christ (Romans 8:18-23; I Corinthians 15:51-53).

Being filled with the Spirit is for all of life. Every person in the home needs the filling of the Spirit in order to be what God desires for him to be (Ephesians 5:18-6:4).

Being a Spirit-filled Christian is not an option; it is a command (Ephesians 5:18).

At the moment we are saved, we are sealed by the Holy Spirit (Ephesians 4:30).

We receive the earnest of the Spirit at the time we are saved (II Corinthians 1:22, 5:5).

At the moment we believe on Christ, the Holy Spirit does everything that we need to keep us safe and secure in Jesus Christ. But the enabling we need to live the Christian life day by day is provided by the filling of the Spirit (Ephesians 5:18; Galatians 5:22-23).

As Christians, our bodies are the temple of the Holy Spirit (I Corinthians 6:19-20).

Among Christians, there are those who are carnal and those who are spiritual. We can live a spiritual life by living a Spirit-filled life (I Corinthians 3:1-4).

The evidence of Spirit filling is not speaking in some strange language; it is speaking boldly in the name of the Lord Jesus Christ (Acts 4:31).

The ministry of the Holy Spirit in this world is to magnify the Lord Jesus Christ. As we are filled with the Spirit, our lives magnify the Lord (John 15:26-27; Acts 4:8-13).

We must thirst for God if we are going to be filled with His Spirit (John 7:37-39).

In order to be filled with the Spirit, we must believe God for this promise (John 7:38).

We should ask God for the filling of the Spirit (Luke 11:11-13).

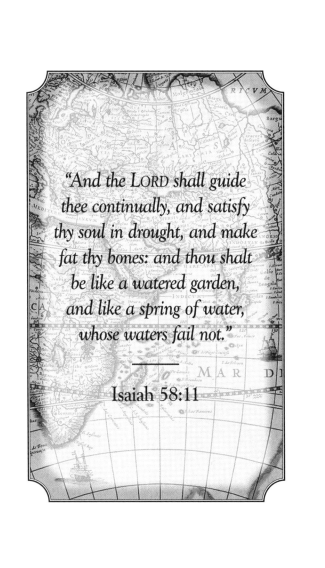

"And the LORD shall guide thee continually, and satisfy thy soul in drought, and make fat thy bones: and thou shalt be like a watered garden, and like a spring of water, whose waters fail not."

Isaiah 58:11

CHAPTER EIGHT

THE LORD IS OUR GUIDE

s it possible to have God's guidance for our lives? In Isaiah 58 the prophet was called upon to cry out against the sins of the people. This is always more difficult than bringing a message of comfort. Whether it is crying out against the sins of the people or bringing a message of comfort, the greatest thing is doing whatever God wants us to, and bringing the message He has laid upon our hearts to bring.

In Isaiah 58:11 the Bible says, *"And the LORD shall guide thee continually, and satisfy thy soul in drought, and make fat thy bones: and thou shalt be like a watered garden, and like a spring of water, whose waters fail not."*

Notice the first expression in this verse, *"The LORD shall guide thee continually."* There are other beautiful things He adds, such as *"...satisfy thy soul in drought...."* When everything else is dried up, we will not be. This is a great promise.

He says, *"...make fat thy bones...."* This speaks of having healthy bones. God said He would make our bones fat. The factory for life is in the marrow of the bones. God says, "I will make you healthy as you allow Me to guide you."

He says, *"...and thou shalt be like a watered garden...."* My wife and I love to see gardens that people have grown. When the rains come, they become so beautiful. God says that our lives will be like a well-watered garden. It will not be parched and half grown. I would like my life to be like a well-watered garden.

He then says, *"...like a spring of water, whose waters fail not."* A spring continually brings forth cool, wonderful, thirst-quenching water. All of this is connected to God's guiding.

In this chapter, Isaiah started crying out against the sins of the people. He said that they bowed their heads, but their hearts were not broken. He then told what God expected of them. From verses eight to twelve Isaiah declares to us the characteristics of a blessed life. Then, in Isaiah 59:1-2 we read,

> *Behold, the LORD's hand is not shortened, that it cannot save; neither his ear heavy, that it cannot hear: but your iniquities have separated between you and your God, and your sins have hid his face from you, that he will not hear.*

I want to emphasize this expression, *"The LORD shall guide thee."* Is it possible to have supernatural guidance in our lives? The answer to this question is yes. We need to be very sure that we are being led of the Lord.

There is a God in heaven who loves us. He loves us so much that He proved His love by sending His Son to bleed and die for our sins. Jesus Christ paid our sin debt on the cross. We can go to anyone in any place in all the world and declare to that particular person, "Christ died for you." We can be confident of this because the Bible says in John 3:16, *"For God so loved the world, that he gave his only begotten Son, that whosoever believeth in him should not perish, but have everlasting life."* The Bible says in Hebrews 2:9 that the Lord Jesus Christ tasted death for every man. He paid every man's sin debt. We can declare to people that Christ died for them.

The Lord Jesus Christ tasted death for every man. We can declare to people that Christ died for them.

The Lord loves us and He wants to lead us. He wants to be our guide. He desires what is best for us, even beyond what we could ever comprehend. The Word of God says that, when we pray, God is able to give us *"exceeding abundantly above all that we ask or think"*(Ephesians 3:20). God can do more through us than ever imagined if we allow Him to guide us.

In Psalm 23:3 we find an interesting and powerful expression. The Bible says, *"He restoreth my soul: he leadeth me in the paths of righteousness for his name's sake."* Notice the three words, *"He leadeth me."* As a shepherd would lead his sheep, and find places to graze and water His sheep, as he would gently care for his flock and each individual sheep in that flock, *"He leadeth me."* This should be more than just an expression we read in the Bible; it should be something that is at work in our lives. We know that our heavenly Father leads us. This is not just for the pastor; the Lord wants to lead all His children.

As a young person, God can lead you into what you are supposed to do with your life. As a young person, God can lead you to the person you are supposed to spend the rest of your life with as a husband or wife. You can know God's will. When you come to a great crisis in your life and you wonder which way to turn, God can lead you in that hour of crisis and show you, "This is the right way. Walk this way. This is the way of My choosing for your life." When difficult decisions come about our health, our employment, or whatever situation in life, God can and will lead us if we allow Him. We can each say, *"He leadeth me."* We should ask ourselves if we really desire God's leading. Do we really want the Lord to lead our lives? We are going to make a big mess of our lives if we do not allow Him to lead.

In 1892 Charles Haddon Spurgeon, "the prince of preachers," died in Mentone, France. He preached his last sermon at the great Metropolitan Tabernacle in London in June of 1891. Then in February of 1892, he died, after being bedridden for eleven days.

When he died, he left the largest congregation in the world without a leader. Seven thousand people were meeting every Sunday in that church. Spurgeon had the privilege of preaching to them and leading them. When he died, they had no pastor. There arose within the Metropolitan Tabernacle, that great Baptist church, a controversy over who would be the pastor.

Spurgeon's brother, James, was a co-pastor, but he also pastored another church while assisting Spurgeon in the work of the Metropolitan Tabernacle. Spurgeon had two sons, twin boys, Thomas and Charles. Thomas was weak physically, but strong spiritually. His father had sent him to New Zealand for his health years before. There was a famous American preacher by the name of A. T. Pierson who was a favorite preacher at the Tabernacle. He had been invited by Spurgeon to fill the pulpit when Spurgeon was suffering with his health. There were many people who wanted Pierson to become the pastor of the Tabernacle, but Pierson was a Presbyterian and refused to become a Baptist. Spurgeon's brother, James, made a play for the church, but James was not much of a preacher, and the people did not want him to lead them. There was tremendous controversy in the church about who was to be the pastor.

After his father's death, Thomas returned from New Zealand and was preaching at the Tabernacle. The people knew he was a preacher, but they were really not profoundly interested in him as a pastor in the beginning. They ended up calling him as the pastor of the Tabernacle, and Thomas served as the pastor of his father's church for fourteen years. After the vote was taken to make Thomas the pastor of the great Metropolitan Tabernacle in London, Thomas pulled a letter from his pocket that he had carried for nine years. He had never allowed anyone to read it, but nine years earlier his father had written him and said, "Get well and come to the Tabernacle and take my place as the pastor." When he read that note to the church, after they called him, they began shouting, waving their handkerchiefs, crying and weeping all over that great Tabernacle. In one voice they proclaimed, "We have not only done what we believed to be the Master's will, we have said 'yes' to what our dear Spurgeon wanted us to do."

As I thought about that story, I thought of the faith that young man had to hold that letter unread, without any mention of it until after everything was done. He could have used the letter. He could have pried the people with it. He could have forced the door open. He could have shown the leaders. But he never made one mention of it. He just knew in his heart that God's will would be done. He waited on the Lord to guide. The way he handled that one thing confirmed to that congregation that they had truly called a man of God as their pastor because he had the faith to trust God to guide him.

Perhaps the one thing that betrays us is that we talk so much and we work so hard to manipulate and plan to get things done for our benefit. Seldom do we ever really wait on God to lead us and do what only God can do. Is it really possible for the Lord to guide us? With all of my heart, I believe it is.

THE WITNESS WITHIN

The Lord speaks to us through His Word, through circumstances, and through other Christians. However, we have the witness of the Holy Spirit who comes to indwell us and gives us divine impressions about what we are to do with our lives.

In John chapter three we read of the conversation that Christ had with Nicodemus. Nicodemus came to Him under the cover of darkness to know more of eternal life. The Bible says in John 3:1-6,

> *There was a man of the Pharisees, named Nicodemus, a ruler of the Jews: the same came to Jesus by night, and said unto him, Rabbi, we know that thou art a teacher come from God: for no man can do these miracles that thou doest, except God be with him. Jesus answered and said unto him, Verily, verily, I say unto thee, Except a man be born again, he cannot see the kingdom of God. Nicodemus saith unto him, How can a man be born when he is old? can he enter the second time into his mother's womb, and be born? Jesus answered, Verily, verily, I say unto thee, Except a man be born of water and of*

the Spirit, he cannot enter into the kingdom of God. That which is born of the flesh is flesh; and that which is born of the Spirit is spirit.

Notice the expression, *"that which is born of the Spirit is spirit."* We need a spiritual birth. At the moment of salvation, when we ask God to forgive our sin and by faith receive Jesus Christ, the Lord in the Person of the Holy Spirit comes to live within us. We must have this witness within us in order for God to guide us.

In John 16:13 our Lord said to His troubled disciples, when He was explaining to them that He was going away, *"Howbeit when he, the Spirit of truth, is come, he will guide you into all truth."* First the Spirit of truth, the Holy Spirit, must come to indwell us; then He will guide us into all truth.

In I Thessalonians 5:23 the Bible says, *"And the very God of peace sanctify you wholly; and I pray God your whole spirit and soul and body be preserved blameless unto the coming of our Lord Jesus Christ."* Notice the words *"spirit and soul and body."* The Lord declares that we are spirit, soul, and body. We are not just body, but spirit, soul, and body. I tell people often when they are getting married, "If you want to be one in the Lord, you will be more than just one in body." The overwhelming emphasis of the world is on the body. There is more to oneness than bodily oneness.

In body, we have a physical instrument in which God has given us to function; but within our body there is a soul. In our soul we have intellect, emotion, and will. We also have a spirit. In our spirit we have a conscience. Every person without Jesus Christ is dead spiritually. We cannot be led of the Spirit of God if we are dead spiritually. If the Lord is going to guide our lives by His Spirit, we must have experienced a spiritual birth. The Holy Spirit comes to indwell the believer when he is born again.

People say, "I am a Christian. When I die, I am going to heaven." This is wonderful. Thank God for it. But what about here and now? The Lord desires to guide us now. He wants us to be the people He created us and saved us to be. He does this from the witness within us once we are born of the Spirit of God.

The Lord declares that we are spirit, soul, and body.

We should want God to guide us, not only in what we call the big decisions of life, but in every decision. I have prayed often, "Lord, guide me in the smallest matters in life. The things I consider to be almost insignificant, God, guide me in these things. Lord, show me in the tiniest of things what it is You want for my life." This is where we go off course. As we look out and see human wreckage, we know that somewhere they veered off course just a little bit. This is why it is so important for God to guide us.

The Bible says in Proverbs 20:27, *"The spirit of man is the candle of the LORD, searching all the inward parts of the belly."* Notice the word *"candle."* Our spirit is called the candle of the Lord. Remember that we are spirit, soul, and body. Our spirit is a candle. If I held a candle in my hand, and it had never been lit, it would still be a candle. If I light it, it would still be a candle. It can be a candle without flame and light or a candle with flame and light, but it is still a candle.

Our spirit, as the candle of the Lord, is not lit until we are saved. At the moment the Spirit of God comes to indwell us, our spirit is lit, and there is the witness of the Lord living in us to guide us. We must be born again. There must be spiritual life. There are many folks we try to instruct, and help, and guide, who just keep going in the wrong direction. I think at some point in time they must inevitably ask themselves if their candle has ever been lit. They must ask themselves if they have been born again.

The Bible says, *"The LORD shall guide thee."* Psalm twenty-three says, *"He leadeth me."* If this is going to happen, there must be a witness within.

THE WILLINGNESS TO OBEY

How does God make us willing to be led? There must be a willingness to obey, to be guided. Where does this come from?

In Psalm 37:1 the Bible says, *"Fret not thyself because of evildoers, neither be thou envious against the workers of iniquity."* For most of us, it is after we go through awful struggles, battles, and inward confusion that we wave the white flag and say, "All right, Lord, I am willing." There is struggling that takes place. After salvation, we are people of two natures, old and new. This means that there is going to be a battle. Once we have trusted the Lord Jesus as Savior, there is a conflict. Who wins the conflict? God is able and He is ultimately victorious, but who wins in each particular conflict? How does God bring us to a willingness? He breaks us. He touches our lives. He uses something that we think is a problem that is not really the problem at all; it is the tool God uses to solve our problem. The problem is not the

Our spirit is called the candle of the Lord.

person we are wrestling with, or the thing that we think is staggering us. The real problem is that we have not come to the place where we say, "Lord, not my will, but Thine be done." Is it a child God uses? Is it a job God uses? Often we try to fix the circumstances, while God is trying to work on us and in us to bring us to the place where we are willing for God to guide us.

God's Word continues in verses one through four,

> *Fret not thyself because of evildoers, neither be thou envious against the workers of iniquity. For they shall soon be cut down like the grass, and wither as the green herb. Trust in the LORD, and do good; so shalt thou dwell in the land, and verily thou shalt be fed. Delight thyself also in the LORD; and he shall give thee the desires of thine heart.*

We are not first to delight in things, but rather to delight in the Lord. He said, *"Delight thyself also in the LORD."* He did not say to delight in the desires of your heart, but in the Lord. This verse means that when we come to the place where we delight in the Lord, then God puts in us the desires He wants us to have. This brings us into harmony with His will. We must first delight in the Lord.

How do we get to the place of delighting in the Lord? As we find that He is all we have and all we need, then we can delight in Him. When He shakes us up, and our lives fall apart, then we come to the place where we know that all we have left is God and He is enough. Then we say, "Lord, I delight in You." He does something beautiful then. He puts His desires in us, and we start wanting from Him what He has always wanted for us. He brings us into harmony with His will.

Psalm 37:5-8 states,

> *Commit thy way unto the LORD; trust also in him; and he shall bring it to pass. And he shall bring forth thy righteousness as the light, and thy judgment as the noonday. Rest in the LORD, and wait patiently for him: fret not thyself because of him who prospereth in his way, because of the man who bringeth wicked devices to pass. Cease from anger, and forsake wrath: fret not thyself in any wise to do evil.*

We get so worked up that we want to take things into our own hands. God said to cease from anger. We are to forsake that attitude. In the final part of verse eight He says, *"Fret not thyself in any wise to do evil."* Most of us think that evil means to go out and do something dirty or wrong. Evil, in this context, is just saying, "Lord, I am going to take care of this myself." The Lord works in our lives to bring us to the place of willingness. He gets us ready to be guided. He cannot guide us until we are ready to be guided.

As I look back across my life at how many things I have gone through, I realize that these things are not big troubles. These are the things God used to help me realize that I need Him to guide me. The big trouble was in not allowing God in the beginning to guide me.

When we get willing, God will guide us. The Bible says in John 7:17, *"If any man will do his will, he shall know of the doctrine, whether it be of God, or whether I speak of myself."* The great struggle is to become willing. We like to say that we are willing just because we are Christians. We like to say that we are willing because we are in church. We like to say that we are willing because we are expected to be willing. However, many times we are not truly willing.

Human understanding and human wisdom will bring us into conflict with God. The way we want to solve our difficulties brings us into conflict with God. It may be that God allows us to use one of those ideas later, but first we must come to the place where we say, "Lord, I am willing to say that I do not know the answers. I want You to guide me."

Human understanding and human wisdom will bring us into conflict with God.

God wants to guide all of us, but few of us are really guided by the Lord. Notice the first expression of John 7:17, *"If any man will do his will, he shall know..."* We should say, "Lord, I will obey You. Show me anything and I will obey You." He wants to bring us to this place of willingness.

THE WAY GOD GUIDES

The way God guides us is very simple–He guides us one step at a time. This is why we have to give such attention to little things. The Bible says in Psalm 119:105, *"Thy word is a lamp unto my feet, and a light unto my path."* We cannot see the entire path.

People come to us and say, "Do you have a ten-year plan? Do you have a fifteen-year plan? Do you have a twenty-year plan?" They want us to think about where we are going to be in so many years. We do have to think about the future, but God is going to guide us one step at a time, one day at a time. *"Thy word is a lamp unto my feet, and a light unto my path."* All we are going to see is the next step.

We think we want to see all that lies ahead for us. We say, "Dear God, move the curtain and show me everything." If He did, we would crumble. We would melt for fear.

Rudyard Kipling crossed the Atlantic with his daughter. He nicknamed her Jo. On the trip, they played on the deck of the boat. Not long after the journey the little daughter died. He was quoted as saying, "If I had known what was lying ahead with that little girl, I could never have enjoyed the trip with her across the ocean. God did not roll back the curtain and let me see it all. I could not have borne that burden."

We do have to think about the future, but God is going to guide us one step at a time, one day at a time. God leads us each step of the way, and He gives us grace each step of the way to deal with what He gives us.

We think we want to see more than we need to see. If I had been told thirty years ago when I started out as a preacher that I would be doing what I am doing today, I would have said, "Not me." However, God leads us each step of the way, and He gives us grace each step of the way to deal with what He gives us. We need to say, "Lord, show me the next step."

The Bible says very plainly in James 1:5, *"If any of you lack wisdom, let him ask of God, that giveth to all men liberally, and upbraideth not; and it shall be given him."* We need to simply ask.

There must be a witness within. There must be a willingness to allow God to guide us. This is a struggle. We must come to the place where we say, "Lord, I will do Your will." The moment we say we will do it, He will let us know what the next step is. The way He leads us is one step at a time, as we ask Him for wisdom.

TRUTHS TO REMEMBER

The Lord loves us and desires to lead us (John 3:16; Isaiah 58:11).

We need to be sure that we are being guided by the Lord in life (Isaiah 58:11; Proverbs 3:5-6).

God can do more through us than we have ever imagined if we allow Him to guide us (Ephesians 3:20).

As a shepherd leads his sheep, gently caring for their every need, so the Lord leads His children (Psalm 23:3).

The indwelling Holy Spirit of God guides us and gives us divine impressions about what we are to do with our lives (John 16:13).

God says that we are spirit, soul, and body. If the Lord is going to guide us by His Spirit, we must have experienced a spiritual birth (I Thessalonians 5:23; John 3:3-6).

We should want God to guide us, not only in what we call the big decisions of life, but in every decision (Proverbs 3:5-6).

The Lord works in our lives to bring us to the place of willingness. He cannot guide our lives until we are willing to obey (John 7:17).

When we find that Christ is all we have and all we need, then we can delight in Him. As we delight in Him, He puts His desires in us, and we start wanting from Him what He has always wanted for us (Psalm 37:1-8).

God does not reveal all that lies ahead for us. He guides us one step at a time (Psalm 119:105).

We need to ask God for wisdom to take the next step He has for our lives (James 1:5).

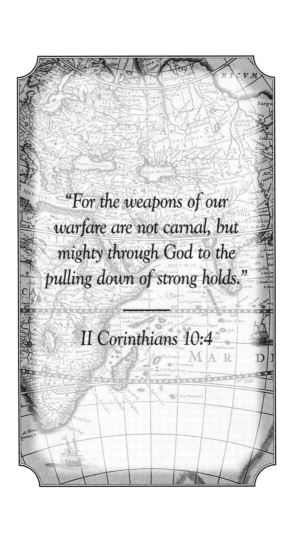

"For the weapons of our
warfare are not carnal, but
mighty through God to the
pulling down of strong holds."

II Corinthians 10:4

CHAPTER NINE

WE ARE ENGAGED IN A SPIRITUAL WARFARE

The Bible clearly teaches that we are engaged in a warfare. Once, after hearing me speak about the conditions that we are having to deal with in our country, my oldest son, who was a teenager at the time, said to me, "Dad, it's good to hear all these things, but don't ever stop telling us what can be done about it."

Often there is a feeling of helplessness that grips people when dealing with problems. We are in a war, but the weapons of our warfare are mighty.

The Bible says in II Corinthians 10:3-5,

> *For though we walk in the flesh, we do not war after the flesh: (for the weapons of our warfare are not carnal, but mighty through God to the pulling down of strong holds;) casting down*

imaginations, and every high thing that exalteth itself against the knowledge of God, and bringing into captivity every thought to the obedience of Christ.

Someone recently gave me a book entitled, *Famous American Letters.* One letter in the book was written from President Eisenhower to his wife Mamie on April 16, 1944, while he was leading our forces in Europe during World War II.

He wrote,

> How I wish this cruel business of war could be completed quickly. Entirely aside from longing to return to you (and stay there) it is a terribly sad business to total up the casualties each day—even in an air war—and to realize how many youngsters are gone forever. A man must develop a veneer of callousness that lets him consider such things dispassionately; but he can never escape a recognition of the fact that back home the news brings anguish and suffering to families all over the country. Mothers, fathers, brothers, sisters, wives and friends must have a difficult time preserving any comforting philosophy and retaining any belief in the eternal rightness of things. War demands real toughness of fiber—not only in the soldiers that must endure, but in the homes that must sacrifice their best.

Many people have given their lives in American wars. In World War I, 116,780 Americans were killed. In World War II, there were 408,306 Americans killed. In the Korean War, there were 54,246 Americans killed. In the Vietnam War, there were 58,219 Americans killed.

War is a terrible thing. We have supported every noble effort this country has been involved in, and we will continue to do so. But all of God's people are engaged in a warfare just as seriously and earnestly as men and women in military service.

WE HAVE JESUS CHRIST AS OUR CAPTAIN

The Bible says that our warfare is a spiritual warfare. We have a captain. His name is Jesus Christ. In the last book of the Bible, Christ says, *"I am he that liveth, and was dead; and, behold, I am alive for evermore, Amen; and have the keys of hell and of death"* (Revelation 1:18).

As we think about war letters, think about this one. Here is a war letter. *"For God so loved the world, that he gave his only begotten Son, that whosoever believeth in him should not perish, but have everlasting life"* (John 3:16).

The greatest conflict ever fought on this earth was the conflict Christ waged against the Devil and sin when He bled and died for our sin on Calvary's cross. The Bible says, *"For he hath made him to be sin for us, who knew no sin; that we might be made the righteousness of God in him"* (II Corinthians 5:21).

Let us never tire of telling the story of how Christ came to earth to be born in Bethlehem's manger. The Lord Jesus did not begin in Bethlehem. He had no beginning. God became a man without ceasing to be God. Mary brought forth into the world the virgin-born Son of God sent by God the Father. The Lord

Jesus said, *"For the Son of man is come to seek and to save that which was lost"* (Luke 19:10).

The Lord Jesus told a parable while He was on this earth about a shepherd with a hundred sheep. Ninety-nine of them were safe and one was lost. He said that the shepherd did everything that was necessary to find that one lost sheep.

In order for God to find us, He sent His Son to Calvary. When Christ went to the cross, He did not go for Himself; He went for us. The Bible says in Isaiah 53:5, *"But he was wounded for our transgressions, he was bruised for our iniquities: the chastisement of our peace was upon him; and with his stripes we are healed."*

> *He is the only One who could pay our debt because He owed no debt of His own.*

Jesus Christ was spat upon and crowned with thorns. He was beaten until His back was ripped open and bleeding. A robe of mockery was placed on His shoulders. Christ went to Calvary. Cruel spikes were driven into His hands and feet as He was nailed to a cross. The Son of God bled and died there.

Someone dares to ask, "Why?" Again the Bible says, *"For God so loved the world..."* You and I are part of the world. *"...that he gave his only begotten Son, that whosoever believeth in him should not perish, but have everlasting life"* (John 3:16).

Look again at Calvary and see this. The Bible says in Hebrews 2:9, *"But we see Jesus, who was made a little lower than the angels for the suffering of death, crowned with glory and honour; that he by the grace of God should taste death for every man."* This is the sinless Son of God who knew no sin, who owed no sin debt.

So why did Jesus Christ die? He is the only Person who ever walked this earth who owed no sin debt. He did not have to die. He is the only One who could pay our debt because He owed no debt of His own. So He went to the cross.

The billows of God's wrath rolled on the Son of God as He became sin for us. God the Father struck His own Son on the cross. He suffered our punishment. He made our payment. He died for you and for me. He was buried and rose from the dead.

Jesus Christ said, *"I am he that liveth, and was dead; and, behold, I am alive for evermore"* (Revelation 1:18). Our hope is in the Lord. He is the victorious One. He has conquered every foe.

> *The only way to get to heaven is to personally trust in God's Son, the Lord Jesus Christ.*

The Bible says, *"And as it is appointed unto men once to die, but after this the judgment"* (Hebrews 9:27). When we go through the door of death, we are going to meet a holy God. Every person will spend eternity either in heaven or hell. The only way to get to heaven is to personally trust in God's Son, the Lord Jesus Christ.

The writer of the great hymn "It Is Well With My Soul" had it right when he wrote, "My sin not in part, but the whole is nailed to the cross and I bear it no more."

I do not have to fear death. The Lord Jesus spoke the truth when He said, *"I am the resurrection, and the life: he that believeth in me, though he were dead, yet shall he live: and whosoever liveth and believeth in me shall never die"* (John 11:25-26).

WE HAVE AN ARMY

In our warfare, our captain is Jesus Christ. In this warfare, we have an army. This army consists of more than individual Christians.

When the Lord Jesus came into the coasts of Caesarea Philippi in Matthew 16:13-18, He asked His disciples,

> *Whom do men say that I the Son of man am? And they said, Some say that thou art John the Baptist: some, Elias; and others, Jeremias, or one of the prophets. He saith unto them, But whom say ye that I am? And Simon Peter answered and said, Thou art the Christ, the Son of the living God. And Jesus answered and said unto him, Blessed art thou, Simon Bar-jona: for flesh and blood hath not revealed it unto thee, but my Father which is in heaven. And I say also unto thee, That thou art Peter, and upon this rock I will build my church; and the gates of hell shall not prevail against it.*

The Lord's army is the local church. Each local church is to be a base camp training people to do the work of God worldwide. Every local, Bible-believing church is to train an army of soldiers for the Lord to do God's work.

We are after men for Christ. Every church must be a mighty army that moves forward to do the work of God. If God's Word is true and there is a real heaven and a real hell, then the army of God in every local church should be moving out into the community doing the work of the Lord, telling people the Good News of Jesus Christ.

Our country is in a deplorable situation spiritually. In September, 2001, the *USA Today* reported that 325,000 young people in America are used each year in pornography. Fifty-two thousand of these children, according to the report done by the University of Pennsylvania, have been thrown away by their parents. Think of how the Devil is waging war in our country!

God has a mighty army. This army is every church that will rise up and be what it should be. The Lord's army, the local church, must move to action in this warfare.

We Have an Enemy

We have an enemy. He is none other than the Devil. In Ephesians 6:10-12 the Bible says,

> *Finally, my brethren, be strong in the Lord, and in the power of his might. Put on the whole armour of God, that ye may be able to stand against the wiles of the devil. For we wrestle not against flesh and blood, but against principalities, against powers, against the rulers of the darkness of this world, against spiritual wickedness in high places.*

Our enemy, the Devil, has two other enemies standing with him–the world and the flesh. Together, the world, the flesh, and the Devil battle against God and God's people.

The Bible says in Ezekiel 14:14, *"Though these three men, Noah, Daniel, and Job, were in it, they should deliver but their own souls by their righteousness, saith the Lord GOD."* As God dealt with Israel and spoke about the judgment He had brought on the land, He used these three men as examples to the people. These men were victorious against all odds.

Noah, in particular, did battle with the world and came out victorious. Daniel did battle with the flesh in an unusual way. In an hour of great temptation, he came out victorious. Job did battle with the Devil. When the Devil was unleashed on him, Job came through in victory. We face these same enemies today.

We must never forget that there is a spirit world. Among the created beings, there are untold numbers of angels created by the Lord. The names of some of these angels are given to us in the Bible. For example, we know that Michael is the archangel. He is the only angel in the Bible referred to as *"the"* archangel. We also read about the angel Gabriel; and then, of course, there is Lucifer.

The Lord's army is the local church. Each local church is to be a base camp training people to do the work of God worldwide.

Lucifer is referred to in Isaiah 14 as the *"son of the morning."* He is the angelic being who rebelled against God and is now known as the Devil. He influences, not only individuals, but also nations. He leads a force of angels who rebelled with him. His judgment has already been determined. According to Revelation 20:10, he will be cast into the lake of fire. His followers will be tormented with him. We praise God for the angels who remained true to the Lord and minister to us just as they ministered to Christ as He yielded to the Father's will in Luke 22:42.

Are we really warring against flesh and blood? No, not on this spiritual front. We battle against the wiles of the Devil.

We Have Weapons

We have need of these weapons. The Bible says, *"For the weapons of our warfare are not carnal, but mighty."* God speaks about a different kind of weapon.

In Hebrews 4:12 the Bible says,

> *For the word of God is quick, and powerful,*
> *and sharper than any twoedged sword, piercing*
> *even to the dividing asunder of soul and spirit,*
> *and of the joints and marrow, and is a discerner*
> *of the thoughts and intents of the heart.*

The Bible is our weapon. This sounds rather simplistic to people, but people need God's Word. We have weapons and we need to use them.

We are living in a biblically illiterate world. Often I am amazed as I talk with young people and find out how little of the Bible they know. There was a time when the language of the Bible could be heard on the street. People would use terms such as, "He's driving like Jehu" or "That woman looks like a Jezebel" or "This reminds me of David and Goliath" or "He's like one of the Lord's disciples" or "That's the gospel truth." But this language has faded. Instead of the world using the language of the Bible and being familiar with the things of God, the church is using the language of the world and knowing very little about the Bible.

We are not going to win the spiritual warfare until we start using the weapon God has given us. We must use this weapon. The Word of God is our arsenal. There are sixty-six wonderful books in one Book. All of it is the living, eternal Word of God.

The Bible says,

> *All scripture is given by inspiration of God, and is profitable for doctrine, for reproof, for correction, for instruction in righteousness: that the man of God may be perfect, throughly furnished unto all good works* (II Timothy 3:16-17).

All across our land and around the world, we need a revival of Bible reading, Bible preaching, and Bible teaching. This is the great weapon of our warfare.

God's Word teaches us in Ephesians chapter six that we have a great arsenal to use against our enemy. Ephesians 6:13-18 says,

> *Wherefore take unto you the whole armour of God, that ye may be able to withstand in the evil day, and having done all, to stand. Stand therefore, having your loins girt about with truth, and having on the breastplate of righteousness; and your feet shod with the preparation of the gospel of peace; above all, taking the shield of faith, wherewith ye shall be able to quench all the fiery darts of the wicked. And take the helmet of salvation, and the sword of the Spirit, which is the word of God: praying always with all prayer and supplication in the Spirit.*

When observing the technology used by our military, I never cease to be amazed at how we can pinpoint targets. It is fascinating to know that we can send unmanned aircraft to bomb predetermined targets with pinpoint accuracy. It is amazing that we can send aircraft from the continental United States thousands of miles around the world to carry out their bombing mission and come back. It is amazing that through infrared readings, we can detect what is hiding on the ground and underneath the ground, and we can know whether it is a rabbit or a human being. What amazing weaponry we have. What fascinating technology we have.

> *Instead of the world using the language of the Bible and being familiar with the things of God, the church is using the language of the world and knowing very little about the Bible.*

My wife and I have had the privilege of traveling to the Middle East many times. We have talked to many people there. They brag about the weaponry they use to protect their borders.

But the truth is, no country will ever invent more powerful weaponry than God has given His people. The only problem is that we have it piled up, and we are not using it. We are going unarmed into battle against the Devil and his forces when we have all we need for victory at our disposal.

THE TRUTH

Here are our weapons. Verse fourteen of Ephesians six says, *"Stand therefore, having your loins girt about with truth..."* We need truth, not knowledge or information, but truth. We are a land missing the truth, the truth of the Word of God. We need to be willing to bear the stigma, or the "reproach" of being identified as Christians.

Imagine that I got up somewhere in a public meeting, especially in an educational environment, and said, "I don't even believe there is a God. Every man has a right to his opinion," and I rattled off some information about constellations and stars and planets and questioned whether there is a God. There would be people in the audience who call themselves intelligent who would say, "That is a man I'd like to listen to." The Bible says in Romans 1:22, *"Professing themselves to be wise, they became fools."*

Imagine that a man gets up in that same meeting and says, "There is a real heaven and a real hell because the Bible says there is. Jesus Christ is coming back again some day. America needs to be ready to meet God." Someone would say, "Why stick to those old-fashioned biblical values and frighten people?" I am telling you, we need truth in this land. God says truth is a weapon.

THE BREASTPLATE OF RIGHTEOUSNESS

Our weapons are not carnal, but mighty. Our second weapon is found in verse fourteen, *"...having on the breastplate of righteousness."* We need righteousness. We need to be clothed in the righteousness of Jesus Christ.

THE GOSPEL OF PEACE

Verse fifteen says, *"...your feet shod with the preparation of the gospel of peace."* We need the gospel, the Good News. It is a tragic thing to see cities and towns where there are no New Testament churches to go to hopeless, helpless families and tell them about Jesus Christ. Often there are counseling centers and "men of the cloth" talking some religious language. But the great need is to tell people that the only hope they have is in the Person of Jesus Christ.

The Shield of Faith

In verse sixteen, the Bible says we should take *"the shield of faith..."* The shield of faith is a weapon. Faith is believing God and the promises of God.

It is not enough to say to people, "Pick yourself up. Get hold of yourself. Be courageous. Be brave. Face the enemy." Anything short of faith in God is too little because the weapons of our warfare are not carnal.

The Helmet of Salvation

The Bible says we should not only take the shield of faith, but we should also take *"the helmet of salvation..."*

As Christians, we cannot help thinking, with thousands of people dying every day, "How many of them are twice dead? How many of them, when they took their last breath, died without Christ?" What did they need? They needed the helmet of salvation.

The Sword of the Spirit

Verse seventeen also says, *"...the sword of the Spirit..."* The Word of God is a weapon of our warfare. Do you know and love the Word of God? What place does the Bible hold in your life? We must be strong in God's Word.

PRAYING ALWAYS

Another weapon of our warfare is found in verse eighteen, *"Praying always with all prayer..."* This is the weapon of prayer.

I talked to my dear friend Dr. Lee Roberson, who has been in the ministry for longer than most of us have been alive, and said to him, "Dr. Roberson, you've been in the ministry all these years. If you had it all to do over, what would you do differently?"

Without a moment's hesitation, he said to me, "I'd spend much more time in prayer, and I would read the Bible and know more of God's Word than I know now."

Are we not all ashamed of how little we know of the Lord and His Word? I have been a student of the Bible for nearly thirty-five years, but I would not want to be quizzed on it in this hour. There is so much more of God and God's Word I need to hide in my heart, so much more time I need to spend with Him in prayer.

We have an enemy; he is the Devil. We must deal with the Devil by using these weapons. The battlefield is for the souls of men.

TRUTHS TO REMEMBER

We are engaged in a spiritual warfare (II Corinthians 10:4; Ephesians 6:12).

Our captain in this spiritual warfare is the Lord Jesus Christ (Revelation 1:18; Hebrews 2:9-10).

The greatest conflict ever fought on this earth was the conflict Christ waged against the Devil and sin when He bled and died for our sin on Calvary's cross and then rose victoriously from the grave (II Corinthians 5:21; Revelation 1:18).

In this spiritual warfare, the Lord's army is the local church. Each local church is to train an army of soldiers to do God's work (Matthew 16:18).

We have weapons in this spiritual warfare that are not carnal, but mighty (II Corinthians 10:4).

The great weapon of our warfare is the Word of God (Hebrews 4:12; II Timothy 3:16-17; Ephesians 6:17).

Our enemies in this warfare are the world, the flesh, and the Devil (II Timothy 4:10; Galatians 5:17; I Peter 5:8).

The Devil leads a force of angels who rebelled with him against God. They will all be cast into the lake of fire forever (Ephesians 6:12; Revelation 20:10).

The truth of the Word of God is a weapon we use in this spiritual warfare (Ephesians 6:14).

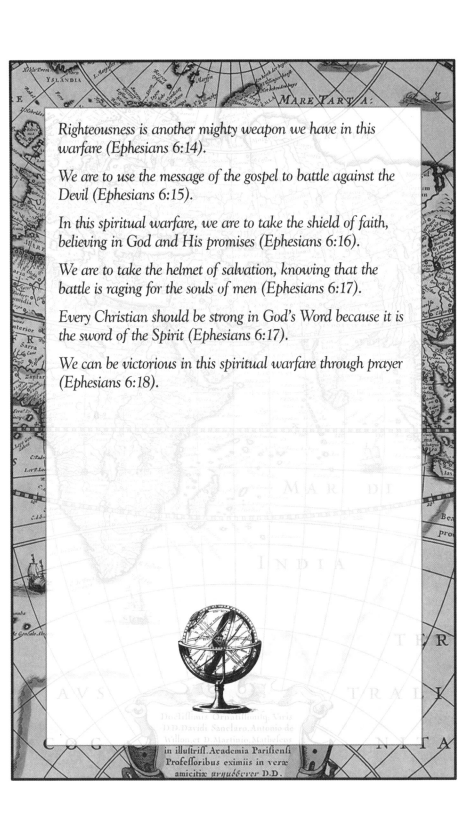

Righteousness is another mighty weapon we have in this warfare (Ephesians 6:14).

We are to use the message of the gospel to battle against the Devil (Ephesians 6:15).

In this spiritual warfare, we are to take the shield of faith, believing in God and His promises (Ephesians 6:16).

We are to take the helmet of salvation, knowing that the battle is raging for the souls of men (Ephesians 6:17).

Every Christian should be strong in God's Word because it is the sword of the Spirit (Ephesians 6:17).

We can be victorious in this spiritual warfare through prayer (Ephesians 6:18).

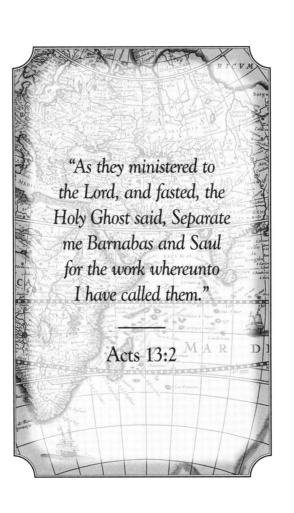

"As they ministered to
the Lord, and fasted, the
Holy Ghost said, Separate
me Barnabas and Saul
for the work whereunto
I have called them."

———

Acts 13:2

CHAPTER TEN

THE WORK OF THE LORD IS OUR MISSION

A dividing line is reached in the wonderful work of God when we arrive at Acts chapter thirteen. Up to this point in the New Testament, the work of the Lord has been centered in the city of Jerusalem. But now, the work moves from that Jewish center to the church in the Gentile city of Antioch, Syria.

The central character among the followers of Christ up to this time has been the apostle Peter. Beginning in Acts chapter thirteen, we come to know more and more of the life and ministry of the apostle Paul. God's work has been centered on one people, the Jews; but now, the Word goes forth to all people, just as God intended for it to do.

In Acts 13:1-4 the Word of God says,

> *Now there were in the church that was at Antioch certain prophets and teachers; as Barnabas, and Simeon that was called Niger, and Lucius of Cyrene, and Manaen, which had been brought up with Herod the tetrarch, and Saul. As they ministered to the Lord, and fasted, the Holy Ghost said, Separate me Barnabas and Saul for the work whereunto I have called them. And when they had fasted and prayed, and laid their hands on them, they sent them away. So they, being sent forth by the Holy Ghost, departed unto Seleucia; and from thence they sailed to Cyprus.*

Note the expression found in the closing part of verse two where the Bible says, *"the work whereunto I have called them."* These are the words of God. Understanding the expression *"called them"* helps us to more thoroughly understand the mind of God.

God is the same yesterday, today, and forever. It is not some new program that the Lord brings to the attention of the church at Antioch. The Word of God says, *"As they ministered to the Lord, and fasted, the Holy Ghost said, Separate me Barnabas and Saul for the work whereunto I have called them."* This is a great missionary effort going forth from this missionary church. Men have made unnecessary divisions in missionary work by referring to some as "home missions" and some as "foreign missions." With God there is only "world evangelism."

When the Lord Jesus was about to ascend to heaven, He declared, *"But ye shall receive power, after that the Holy Ghost is come upon you: and ye shall be witnesses unto me both in*

Jerusalem, and in all Judaea, and in Samaria, and unto the uttermost part of the earth" (Acts 1:8).

What we find in Acts chapter thirteen is the gospel going to the uttermost part of the earth. These men were called missionaries. They went out from a local Bible-believing, Bible-preaching church. It was a program that was church-supported. It was a program that was church-supervised. They were sent out by the local New Testament church.

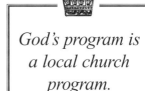

God's program is a local church program.

They came back when they had done a certain measure of the work and told the church that sent them what God had done through their lives and ministry.

God's program is a local church program. You cannot speak of missions, from a biblical perspective, without speaking of the local New Testament church. The Lord Jesus said in Matthew 28:19-20,

> *Go ye therefore, and teach all nations, baptizing them in the name of the Father, and of the Son, and of the Holy Ghost: teaching them to observe all things whatsoever I have commanded you: and, lo, I am with you alway, even unto the end of the world. Amen.*

He was speaking to His disciples. The church started with Christ and His disciples and was empowered at Pentecost. Christ commissioned His church to go into all the world and preach the gospel to every creature. To this point in time, before we arrive at Acts chapter thirteen, the church had not done what the Lord Jesus said they were to do.

The key verse of the book of Acts is found in chapter one and verse eight, and as we read through the book of Acts, we see the work of God in Jerusalem, the work of God in Judea, the work of God in Samaria, and the work of God through the uttermost part of the earth.

When we come to chapter twenty-eight of the book of Acts, there is no ending to the book. There is no conclusion to the book because the work of God to the uttermost part of the earth will not conclude until the last soul has been saved, the bride has been completed, the trumpet sounds, and the Lord Jesus comes for His completed church.

We are living in this book of Acts. We are to continue with the same thing that we find in chapter thirteen. As we examine this wonderful Gentile church of Antioch, this church with a passion and burden for the lost of the world, may God speak to our hearts.

THE MEN IN THE CHURCH

The Bible says in Acts 13:1, *"Now there were in the church that was at Antioch certain prophets and teachers."* These were people who spoke the Word of God with boldness. We find in the Bible a "foretelling" of the things of God and a "forth telling" of the things of God. In our day, we have the completed revelation of God's Word, the Bible, in our hands. This means from the conclusion of the first century until this present moment in time, there has been no new foretelling of things to come. We believe what has been *foretold,* what is yet to take place, and we are involved in *forth telling* the things of God in holy boldness as we preach God's Word.

Prophets and teachers were in this church in Antioch. These men stood strong for God and proclaimed God's Word with holy boldness. These men were soul winners. These men were actively involved in God's work in the church. These men followed up the converts. These men discipled new believers. These men visited the sick and needy. There is no doubt that the church thought these were men that they could not get along without. These were not men in a corner somewhere that no one knew. These were not people who were inactive. These were the prominent leaders, men who were blessed and used of God. They were the people on the very front lines. People looked to them for spiritual leadership in the church. And these were the men that God called from that church to go into all the world and preach the gospel.

Many offer to the Lord what they think they do not need.

Many offer to the Lord what they think they do not need. I hear of pastors getting aggravated at the thought of God calling someone who is actively involved in their ministry. Who do we want to give to Jesus Christ to do His work in all the world? Who do we want to present to our Lord? Notice these men. There are five names mentioned. Each of them has a story to tell. We have some clues from the Bible concerning these men, but much is left to our imagination. Some things about them are not definite but are simply hints that God gives us in His Word.

We know where these men were from. Four of them were Hellenists, Jews who were born outside the Holy Land who spoke the language or the languages of the Gentiles. One was a Jew who was born in the Holy Land. We know this because the Bible tells us where he grew up.

Barnabas

Barnabas was a man who had been greatly used of God. He was from the island of Cyprus. He owned land there. Early on in the work of God, on the day of Pentecost, there were many people saved. The Jews came to Jerusalem for the Feast of Pentecost. Many who got saved did not return immediately to their homes. Because they had not prepared for such a lengthy stay in the city of Jerusalem, great needs arose in the church to care for all the new converts.

This good man who was of the tribe of Levi sold his possession, brought the money he received, and said, "I give this to God to be used to help with the needs of the church."

He identified himself as a man sold out to Jesus Christ. When the apostle Paul, known as Saul of Tarsus, was saved on the road to Damascus, it was Barnabas who befriended Saul and recommended him to the apostles. They thought, no doubt, that Paul might be just a spy, someone trying to find out what they were doing and seeking to bring great persecution to them. After all, Paul was the one who executed the orders to stone Stephen to death. He held the cloaks of those who threw the stones.

It was quite a thing that Barnabas did to influence the other apostles to welcome this converted persecutor into the fellowship of believers.

Simeon

The Bible says, *"Simeon that was called Niger."* The name *Niger* was a nickname given to Simeon. When considering the Gospel according to Mark, we have strong indication that this man is the same man who carried the cross of the Lord Jesus.

The Bible says in Mark 15:21, *"And they compel one Simon a Cyrenian..."* He was from Cyrene, on the north coast of Africa. *"...who passed by, coming out of the country, the father of Alexander and Rufus, to bear his cross."*

At the time John Mark was led of the Spirit of God to write the Gospel record, no doubt the sons of Simon, called Niger, were prominently known in the church. I think this is the reason their names were given. When the reader would read this Gospel record, he would read that this was the Simon of Cyrene, whose sons were Alexander and Rufus.

In Romans 16:13, Paul mentioned a Rufus. Paul more than likely stayed in the home of this Rufus, referring to the mother of Rufus as one of his mothers who cared for and nurtured him. There is some great connection with this Simon of Cyrene. If he truly was the same man who carried the cross of the Lord Jesus, what a wonderful thought that, in this church in Antioch of Syria, this man was to be a part of what God was doing to get the message of Calvary to the whole world.

LUCIUS

In Acts chapter thirteen, we find a third man. The third man was Lucius of Cyrene. We know very little of this man, but I can imagine Simeon of Cyrene hearing the message of Christ, being won to Christ, leading this man to the Lord, and having great influence upon him.

MANAEN

Fourth we find the name of Manaen. He was the only one of the five who was not a Hellenist, a Jew who was born and reared in the Holy Land. He had been brought up with Herod the Tetrarch, or Herod Antipas as he is sometimes called.

If God touches your heart, if God singles you out to serve Him, it will be greater than anything else you have done to that point in your life.

Manaen grew up, one might even say, as a foster brother with Herod the Tetrarch, who lived in adultery and whose sin was brought into the open by the preaching of John the Baptist. Because of this, Herod murdered John the Baptist.

Here we find Manaen, according to Scripture, the same man brought up with Herod the Tetrarch, as a leader, prophet and teacher in this great missionary church at Antioch.

This speaks about the amazing grace of God. Oh, what God can do! One man becomes a Christ-denying murderer. The other man growing up with him becomes a follower of the Lamb of God.

SAUL

Then the Bible says, *"...and Saul."* The Spirit of God gave the physician Luke these words to pen as he wrote this record of the acts of the Holy Spirit in the lives of God's children, and he adds, *"and Saul."* These were mighty men, leaders, prominent men in the church.

The Bible says, *"As they ministered to the Lord, and fasted, the Holy Ghost said, Separate me Barnabas and Saul for the work whereunto I have called them."* All five of these men were being blessed and used of God. These men were needed in the church to get God's work done. These men were relied upon to

THE WORK OF THE LORD IS OUR MISSION

do a mighty work for the Lord in the church in Antioch. These men knew Jesus Christ and were sold out to Him. God said, "I am going to take Barnabas and Saul."

No doubt when that message came to some, they thought, "This is like cutting the arm off our church. But we must think that God has an even greater work for them to do."

If God touches your heart, if God singles you out to serve Him, it will be greater than anything else you have done to that point in your life.

THE MINISTRY IN THE CHURCH

Notice the language of Scripture. The Bible says in verse two, *"As they ministered to the Lord, and fasted."* This sounds a little strange to some people, *"ministered to the Lord."*

Quite frankly, we do not think often that our ministry is to the Lord. We think our ministry is going to the hospital to see someone, going to the nursing home to visit someone, going across town to make a call, or trying to win someone to Christ.

We think of our ministry as a ministry to people. But the primary interest here is not ministering to people; it is ministering to the Lord. What does this mean? It means that we should not offer anything to the people of God or to a lost and dying world until we have first offered it to God. I should not offer myself to others until I have offered myself to God. I should not offer a message to others until first I have brought it to the Lord and said, "Lord, are You pleased with this? Does this honor You?"

Singers should not offer a song to a congregation until they have offered that song to the Lord. We should ask ourselves, "Is God pleased with this? Does this glorify the Lord?" These Christians in Antioch ministered to the Lord. They communed with God. They were serious about this one thing. They wanted to know the mind of Christ concerning the ministry. They wanted to know what God desired for them.

There is something beautiful about the fellowship and harmony of a church, when that church really loves the Lord and follows after God.

On occasion, a young married couple will think as they serve the Lord together that God is dealing with them. Alone, the young man will know God has been speaking to him. The Lord has let him know, "There is something I want you to do with your life." He is trying to think of a way to tell his wife. She loves the Lord. She worships the Lord. She serves the Lord. Then he discovers the most amazing thing. When he finally gets the courage to sit down to talk to her about what God has given him to do, God has also let her know that is what they are to do together.

Where did they get this message? They both got it from the Lord Jesus. They did not get it first from one another. They got it from Christ.

There is something beautiful about the fellowship and harmony of a church when that church really loves the Lord and follows after God. In a church like this, it is a marvelous thing when God's man says, "This is what God wants me to do. This is what God has led me to do." And the people say, "Amen, we have also sought the Lord and we believe this is what God wants us to do."

Who does this? The Lord does this as we minister to Him, as we seek His face. God forbid that we ever get the idea that the only man who hears from heaven is the preacher. The pastor has been called to lead the church, and the Lord is going to speak to the pastor. I find it very difficult to think that God would tell the pastor one thing and tell someone else in the church another thing. But all of us have access to the throne of grace through the Lord Jesus Christ and His precious blood. The Bible teaches the priesthood of every believer. We have *"one mediator between God and men, the man Christ Jesus."* All of us who are saved can approach the Father through His Son. As these men ministered to the Lord, the mind of God was revealed to them.

If I were not a pastor, if I were a layman in the church, I would desire to live a Spirit-filled life in daily communion with God and to know the mind of Christ.

The ministry of the church is a worldwide ministry, and it begins with ministering to the Lord. Find a church that is not taking the message around the world and you will find a church that is not ministering to God. Start with the Lord. Stay with the Lord. Continue in the Lord.

THE MISSION OF THE CHURCH

The Bible says in Acts 13:2-3, *"As they ministered to the Lord, and fasted, the Holy Ghost said, Separate me Barnabas and Saul for the work whereunto I have called them."* What is this work? It is a missionary work.

"And when they had fasted and prayed, and laid their hands on them, they sent them away." When a sacrificial lamb was brought to the priest to be slain as a substitute sacrifice for a person's sins, one of the things the person did in sacrificing the lamb was place his hands on the lamb, identifying himself with that substitutionary sacrifice. This placing on of hands identified him with that substitute, with that work.

In the Bible we find the practice of laying hands on people who are going out to serve God. That whole idea stems from the thought that we are identifying ourselves with the work that those people, on whom we lay our hands, are going to do. We are placing ourselves in the position that is inseparable from what they are doing.

We are not just saying, "We are going to send you out." We are saying, "We are going with you in our prayers and our support. You are here with us. We are there with you. It is one cause, the cause of God, the great cause of Christ, the work of the Holy Spirit. We are working together in this."

> *It is a grand and glorious thing to be a part of the fellowship of a local church.*

They fasted and prayed and laid their hands on these men; then they sent them away. It is a joyous thing to come to church to worship God and to be with people who know God. It is a joyous thing to meet new converts and see people saved. It is a joyous thing to fellowship with believers. It is a grand and glorious thing to be a part of the fellowship of a local church. But there came a day when they did not come to meet there anymore. People came to worship there on the Lord's

Day, and these two were sent away. They were not being punished; they were being blessed and used of God.

The Bible says, *"So they, being sent forth by the Holy Ghost"* (Acts 13:4). It was more than being sent by the church. The Bible says they were sent by the Holy Ghost. Verse three says they were sent by the church.

How were they sent by the church and the Holy Ghost? As the church ministered to the Lord and knew the mind of Christ, they worked together with them in this effort. I Corinthians 3:9 says, *"For we are labourers together with God."* They did the work that the Lord had called them to do.

God promised to Abraham in Genesis 12:3, *"And I will bless them that bless thee, and curse him that curseth thee: and in thee shall all families of the earth be blessed."* When He made this promise to Abraham two thousand years before the birth of Christ, did He mean it?

In Exodus 19:5 the Bible says,

> *Now therefore, if ye will obey my voice indeed, and keep my covenant, then ye shall be a peculiar treasure unto me above all people: for all the earth is mine: And ye shall be unto me a kingdom of priests, and an holy nation.*

A priest represents God to man. He said, "You are going to be a kingdom of priests, telling all men about Me." Did He mean what He said?

In Isaiah chapter forty-nine, the Bible says in verse six,

> *And he said, It is a light thing that thou shouldest be my servant to raise up the tribes of Jacob, and to restore the preserved of Israel: I will*

also give thee for a light to the Gentiles, that thou mayest be my salvation unto the end of the earth.

Did He mean what He said?

In Matthew chapter twenty-eight, the Bible says in verses nineteen and twenty,

> *Go ye therefore, and teach all nations, baptizing them in the name of the Father, and of the Son, and of the Holy Ghost: teaching them to observe all things whatsoever I have commanded you: and, lo, I am with you alway, even unto the end of the world. Amen.*

Acts 1:8 says,

> *But ye shall receive power, after that the Holy Ghost is come upon you: and ye shall be witnesses unto me both in Jerusalem, and in all Judaea, and in Samaria, and unto the uttermost part of the earth.*

> *Friends, spreading the gospel worldwide is not a part of what we do; it is what we do.*

God has always had one program for the whole world. Can you imagine what it meant in that moment, in that church, in that city of Antioch, for those two men to finally begin to do what had always been in the mind of God to get done?

Let us think of the significance of this statement, *"Separate me Barnabas and Saul for the work whereunto I have called them."* The eternal God said, "I have called them. This is what I have said to Abraham. This is what

I have said to Moses. This is what I have said to My prophets. This is what the Lord Jesus said to His disciples. This is it."

Friends, spreading the gospel worldwide is not a *part* of what we do; it is *what* we do. Do you know God? Do you love Him? He has a work He is doing worldwide. Will you have a part in it? Will you minister to the Lord and know the mind of God? Will you pray? Will you give of your means? Will you go? As the Lord touches your heart, will you go to do the work whereunto He has called you?

TRUTHS TO REMEMBER

Christ commissioned His church to go into all the world and preach the gospel to every creature (Matthew 28:19-20; Acts 1:8).

Missionaries are to be sent out by a local New Testament church. They are to be church-supported and church-supervised (Acts 13:1-4).

God often touches the hearts of faithful people and singles them out for His service (Acts 13:2).

Our ministry in the church is not primarily a ministry to people; it is a ministry to the Lord (Acts 13:2).

As we minister to the Lord, the mind of God is revealed to us (Acts 13:2).

The ministry of the church is a worldwide ministry, and it begins with ministering to the Lord (Acts 1:8, 13:2-4).

The work of the Lord is a missionary work. Spreading the gospel worldwide is not a part of what we do; it is what we do (Genesis 12:3; Exodus 19:5; Isaiah 49:6; Matthew 28:19-20; Acts 1:8).

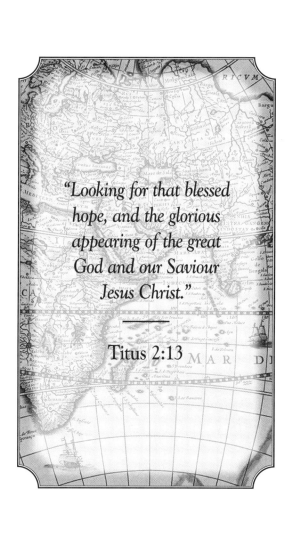

"Looking for that blessed
hope, and the glorious
appearing of the great
God and our Saviour
Jesus Christ."

———

Titus 2:13

CHAPTER ELEVEN

THE COMING OF JESUS CHRIST IS OUR BLESSED HOPE

n the New Testament there are twenty-seven books *"given by inspiration of God,"* that are *"profitable for doctrine, for reproof, for correction, for instruction in righteousness"* (II Timothy 3:16). All the books of the Bible are God-breathed. In the heart of the New Testament there are four pastoral, or personal, epistles– I Timothy, II Timothy, Titus, and Philemon. It is from one of these pastoral epistles that we find the wonderful expression, *"that blessed hope."* The Bible says in Titus 2:11-15,

> *For the grace of God that bringeth salvation hath appeared to all men, teaching us that, denying ungodliness and worldly lusts, we should live soberly, righteously, and godly, in this present world; looking for that blessed hope, and the glorious appearing of the great God and our*

Saviour Jesus Christ; who gave himself for us, that he might redeem us from all iniquity, and purify unto himself a peculiar people, zealous of good works. These things speak, and exhort, and rebuke with all authority. Let no man despise thee.

As we consider the coming of Christ for His own, we know that He is our *"blessed hope."* The world is dying for hope. So few people seem to have any hope. But God says to His children that we have a *"blessed hope."* He is speaking of the coming of the Lord Jesus Christ for His own.

Romans 15:4 tells us, *"For whatsoever things were written aforetime were written for our learning, that we through patience and comfort of the scriptures might have hope."*

Through the Word of God, we find hope. It should not sound strange that a preacher would stand in the pulpit and say, "We believe the Bible; we are Bible-believing people and unashamed of it." On the other hand, it should be strange to find a preacher who would not make that statement. Be a Christian and belong to a Bible-believing church. Our sole authority for faith and practice is the Bible, God's holy Word!

SALVATION

In Titus 2:11 the author speaks of salvation. *"For the grace of God that bringeth salvation hath appeared to all men."* Do you have salvation? Have you trusted the Lord Jesus Christ as your personal Savior? Do you know that you have asked God to forgive your sin and by faith received the Lord Jesus Christ as your Savior? Be certain that you are saved. You can know for sure.

Salvation is not church membership, being baptized, belonging to a Sunday School somewhere, or taking the Lord's

Supper. It is knowing that there was a time in your life when you asked God to forgive your sin and by faith received Jesus Christ as your Savior.

SEPARATION

In Titus 2:11 Paul speaks of salvation. In verse twelve he speaks of separation from the world and unto the Lord. The Bible says, *"Teaching us that, denying ungodliness and worldly lusts, we should live soberly, righteously, and godly, in this present world."* Did you know that what we believe about the Bible has everything to do with the way we live in this world? We behave a certain way because we believe a certain way.

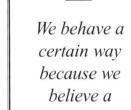

We behave a certain way because we believe a certain way.

Recently I had the opportunity to talk with a lovely young couple. I prayed with them about knowing the Lord as Savior and led them to Christ. This couple prayed and trusted Jesus Christ as their Savior in the privacy of their home.

After they were saved, I talked with them about living for the Lord. I told them that after they got saved, they should live for the Lord out of love for Him and for what He has done for them.

I said to the young man, "You're married, and you are supposed to be with your wife. That's what you're obligated to do. If you spent time with your wife, there are some people who would say, 'Oh, you just do that because you are supposed to do it. You are married to her. You are supposed to spend time with her!' These same people might say of your wife, 'You are married to him so you are supposed to spend time with your husband.' There is a higher motive for a husband and wife spending time together. They spend time together, not simply because they feel as if they are obligated to be together. They love one another and desire to be together."

Some people may look at Christians and say, "Oh, you Christians! You believe the Bible says that you are to live a certain way, that you have to deny worldly lusts. You do that because you think you have to do it!"

This should not be true. There is more to the Christian life than this. We live this way because we love Jesus Christ and we want to be with Him.

When you really love Jesus Christ, people will not have to plead with you to do right. You will be doing right from your heart. When you really love the Lord, it will settle all of this, and you will do what you are supposed to do out of a heart of love for the Lord Jesus Christ.

THE SECOND COMING OF CHRIST

Titus 2:12 speaks of separation. Verse thirteen speaks of the Second Coming of Christ. He is coming again!

The Bible says in verse thirteen, *"Looking for that blessed hope, and the glorious appearing of the great God and our Saviour Jesus Christ."*

No other doctrine in all the Bible has such a transforming effect on the lives of people as the doctrine of the Second Coming of Christ when it is properly understood. Believe by faith that His coming is at hand, that He could come at any moment. He has given us His Word to assure us that He is coming again. The Lord Jesus Christ said in John 14:3, *"I will come again."*

The book of Revelation gives us the account of John's seeing the Lord Jesus Christ. The Revelation was given to John on that rocky isle of Patmos in the Aegean Sea. God rolled back the curtain of heaven, and John saw the Lord Jesus Christ revealed in His holiness and glory. In response, John fell on his face as a dead man.

No other doctrine in all the Bible has such a transforming effect on the lives of people as the doctrine of the Second Coming of Christ.

No one has seen the Lord since. Nevertheless, He is coming again. As Christ stood on the Mount of Olives and ascended into heaven, angels gave a message to His followers that day. The Bible records the message for us in Acts 1:10-11,

> *And while they looked stedfastly toward heaven as he went up, behold, two men stood by them in white apparel; which also said, Ye men of Galilee, why stand ye gazing up into heaven? this same Jesus, which is taken up from you into heaven, shall so come in like manner as ye have seen him go into heaven.*

"This same Jesus" is coming again! He was taken up in the clouds, and He is coming again in the clouds. He was taken up in bodily form, and He is coming again in bodily form. He was taken up recognizably, and He is coming again recognizably. *"This same Jesus"* was taken up from His own and will return to His own. *"This same Jesus"* is coming again!

Over three hundred times in the New Testament alone, God gives us the promise that Jesus Christ is coming again.

A DAY OF RAPTURE

We believe in what we refer to as the Rapture of the church. Someone may say, "That's not a Bible word." True, you will not find the word *rapture* in the Bible. You will not find the word *trinity* in the Bible. You will not find the word *demon* in the Bible. But these are all useful words.

Rapture means "caught up" to be with Him. Our Lord is coming. He is coming for His own, for every believer, without signs. When we are gone, the Antichrist will make his appearance on the earth. The Tribulation period will begin and will last for seven years. At the conclusion of that seven-year period, the Battle of Armageddon will be fought. The Lord Jesus will come in His glory, every eye shall see Him, and His feet shall touch the Mount of Olives. He is coming again!

When Christ comes for His own, it will be a secret coming. It will be *"in the twinkling of an eye"* (I Corinthians 15:52). Someone has estimated that a twinkling is 11/100 of a second. Millions will be missing that quickly.

Some people left on earth will try to explain where the raptured Christians have gone and what is happening. The leader who steps on the stage of human history, the Antichrist, will certainly have an answer for the people because he will lead them when we are gone. The restraining power of the Holy Spirit will be removed. Evil will flood the earth. As children of God, we look for *"that blessed hope."*

There is a verse in Revelation chapter one that speaks of both phases of Christ's coming–His coming secretly and His coming openly. His coming secretly means that He is coming for His church. His coming openly refers to His coming with ten thousands of His saints to execute judgment upon the earth seven years later.

The Bible says in Revelation 1:7, *"Behold, he cometh with clouds."* This is His secret coming. When the trumpet sounds, only the saved will hear the sound of that trumpet. Only the saved will hear the voice of the archangel. Only the saved will hear the shout of God. It will be a secret coming.

> *The restraining power of the Holy Spirit will be removed. Evil will flood the earth.*

Walking through a cemetery, one will not be able to see where any body has been taken because the resurrected body will be like the body of Jesus Christ as He walked through closed doors. The molecular structure of what we see as a solid object today will have no boundary over that body. Remember that the Lord Jesus Christ walked through closed doors in His resurrected body.

Perhaps the newspaper headline will read, "MILLIONS MISSING!!!"

Those without Christ will go to work, and every saved person will not be there. The lost person will wake up in the morning, and every member of his family that was saved will have disappeared during the night. If husband and wife are sleeping together, one saved and the other lost, the saved one will be gone instantly. The Lord Jesus Christ is coming for His own.

Revelation 1:7 also tells us, *"Behold, he cometh with clouds; and every eye shall see him."* The Lord is also coming seven years later when every eye will see Him.

However, let us talk about that first phase, or the part we refer to as the Rapture of the church. Although we may not understand everything, let us acknowledge that we are pre-tribulational and pre-millennial in what we believe about the Bible and the coming of Christ.

Pre-tribulation means that Jesus Christ is coming before the Tribulation. *Pre-millennial* means that He is coming before the millennial reign. The Bible plainly says that He will reign a thousand years upon the earth.

A DAY OF RESURRECTION

The Bible says in Titus 2:13, *"Looking for that blessed hope, and the glorious appearing of the great God and our Saviour Jesus Christ."* Why does God call the appearing of our Savior *"that blessed hope"*? He calls it *"that blessed hope"* because it is a day of resurrection.

People have sometimes wondered how a person can get to heaven without dying. When Jesus Christ comes, some people will have never tasted death. They will go to heaven without dying. The Word of God says in I Corinthians 15:51, *"Behold, I shew you a mystery; We shall not all sleep, but we shall all be changed,..."* This is the mystery. How do you get to the world beyond this world without dying? The only answer is to be alive when Jesus Christ comes.

The Bible continues in I Corinthians 15:52-58,

> *...In a moment, in the twinkling of an eye, at the last trump: for the trumpet shall sound, and the dead shall be raised incorruptible, and we shall be changed. For this corruptible must put on incorruption, and this mortal must put on immortality. So when this corruptible shall have put on incorruption, and this mortal shall have put on immortality, then shall be brought to pass the saying that is written, Death is swallowed up in victory. O death, where is thy sting? O grave, where is thy victory? The sting of death is sin; and the strength of sin is the law. But thanks be to God, which giveth us the victory through our Lord Jesus Christ. Therefore, my beloved brethren, be ye stedfast, unmoveable, always abounding in the work of the Lord, forasmuch as ye know that your labour is not in vain in the Lord.*

God calls this next major event that is to take place on the divine calendar *"that blessed hope"* because it is the day of resurrection.

The other day, my wife and I went by the grave of her father. He was killed in an automobile accident many years ago. His body is in the earth. When his body was placed in the earth, he was not in that body. The apostle Paul, under the inspiration of the Spirit of God, penned these words in II Corinthians 5:8, *"We are confident, I say, and willing rather to be absent from the body, and to be present with the Lord."* When my wife's father died, his soul was set free to be with God. His body was taken by loving, tender hands to a funeral home and prepared for burial. His body is now in a cemetery in Blount County, Tennessee, waiting for the day of resurrection.

When the Lord comes again, my father-in-law is coming with Him, and his body will be resurrected from the earth. No wonder God calls it *"that blessed hope."* That new body is coming up out of the earth to be reunited with him in the air to be ever with the Lord. That new body will be a glorified body, like the body of our Lord Jesus Christ.

A DAY OF REDEMPTION

God calls it *"that blessed hope"* because it is a day of redemption.

Romans 8:18-23 says,

> *For I reckon that the sufferings of this present time are not worthy to be compared with the glory which shall be revealed in us. For the earnest expectation of the creature waiteth for the manifestation of the sons of God. For the creature was made subject to vanity, not willingly, but by reason of him who hath subjected the same in hope, because the creature itself also shall be delivered from the bondage of corruption into the glorious liberty of the children of God. For we know that the whole creation groaneth and travaileth in pain together until now. And not only they, but ourselves also, which have the firstfruits of the Spirit, even we ourselves groan within ourselves, waiting for the adoption, to wit, the redemption of our body.*

We groan and say, "Lord, I want to be better than this. I've done the same thing wrong a hundred times. I don't want to do that again." I like the song the little children sing, "He's Still

Working on Me." He is! He will make me perfect some day, and I will be like Him when I see Him and receive a new body.

No wonder that resurrection chorus found in I Corinthians 15:55 says, *"O death, where is thy sting? O grave, where is thy victory?"* Those who are alive when Jesus Christ comes will never taste death. They will say, *"O death, where is thy sting?"* Those caught up from the grave will look back at the grave and say, *"O grave, where is thy victory?"* God calls it *"that blessed hope"* because it is a day of redemption.

A DAY OF REUNION

I have followed loved ones to a grave and walked out of the cemetery with a broken heart. God says the Second Coming of Christ is *"that blessed hope"* because it is a day of reunion.

In I Thessalonians 4:13-14 the apostle Paul writes under the inspiration of the Spirit of God,

> *But I would not have you to be ignorant, brethren, concerning them which are asleep, that ye sorrow not, even as others which have no hope. For if we believe that Jesus died and rose again, even so them also which sleep in Jesus will God bring with him.*

That is reunion! There is going to be "a meeting in the air in the sweet by and by."

The Bible goes on to say in verses fifteen through seventeen,

211

For this we say unto you by the word of the Lord, that we which are alive and remain unto the coming of the Lord shall not prevent them which are asleep. For the Lord himself shall descend from heaven with a shout, with the voice of the archangel, and with the trump of God: and the dead in Christ shall rise first: then we which are alive and remain shall be caught up together with them in the clouds, to meet the Lord in the air: and so shall we ever be with the Lord.

The eighteenth verse says, *"Wherefore comfort one another with these words."* Every worry I have ever had or ever will have will be over just as soon as the trumpet sounds. It will all be over. Every frustration I have ever had will be gone, just as soon as the trumpet sounds. That is not all of it. I will be reunited with loved ones and friends who have gone on before.

There will be no goodbyes in heaven. It will be a day of reunion.

As a fourteen year-old boy, I followed my father's body to a grave. I never played one high school ball game that my daddy watched. I never ran one touchdown that my daddy was ever able to applaud. I never got dressed in a locker room one time to come out, see his smiling face, and hear him say, "I'm proud of you." I never drove home one time from a revival meeting and had him ask me, "How did the meeting go?"

My dad trusted Christ as his Savior before he died. I will see him at the resurrection. My mother trusted Christ as her Savior before she died. I will see her at the resurrection.

There will be no goodbyes in heaven. It will be a day of reunion.

A DAY OF REJOICING

If you have the idea that going to heaven is just sitting on a cloud somewhere, strumming a harp for the rest of eternity, you are wrong.

God is going to give us plenty to do in this big universe He has created. We will be walking on a street of gold, living in a mansion He has prepared, being with Jesus Christ and the children of God, and rejoicing and praising God forever. No wonder the Lord said it is *"that blessed hope."*

The scoffer said in II Peter 3:4, *"Where is the promise of his coming?"*

The Lord answered in verse nine, *"The Lord is not slack concerning his promise, as some men count slackness; but is longsuffering to us-ward, not willing that any should perish, but that all should come to repentance."*

God is going to keep His Word. Not long after my wife and I were married, we made a trip to Florida. When I was a senior in high school, I lived away from my family. I finished high school in Tennessee, although my family had moved to Florida. I remember so very well talking to my mother on the telephone and telling her that I was coming to see her. I had not seen my mother in a long time. We were so anxious to see one another. She said, "Now, honey, what time are you going to leave?"

I told her.

She replied, "How fast do you think you can drive?"

I said, "I figure so many miles each hour. I will be there at a certain time."

She told me, "Oh, I'm looking forward to seeing you."

I got up really early–I got off to a good start. I started on the road, and I thought all the way, "I'm going to see my mother, brother, and sisters."

I did not know what was going on there. My mother started going outside the house and looking for me much earlier in the day than I could have ever arrived. She would go out and walk around the yard, walk up to the end of the block, walk up to the highway, look down the highway both ways, stand there for a few minutes, and walk back down to the house. Thirty minutes later, she would walk back up to the highway from the house, look both ways, stand there for a little while, and walk back down.

I remember, as if it were yesterday, how I turned the corner from the main road and her house came in view. My mother was standing in the yard. I could not wait to get the car stopped to get out and embrace her. I just wanted to tell her how much I loved her and how much I had missed her.

We will be reunited with loved ones, and we will see Jesus Christ face to face.

I do not know how many times I have thought about heaven, but it has been more times than could be numbered, especially when my heart is hurting too deeply for words. I do not know how many times I have thought about loved ones. I do not know how many times I have thought about people who once put their arms around me and helped me through the years, who are gone to heaven now.

I have tried to imagine what heaven is like, and when I go to sleep somewhere and wake up, not here but there, what it will be like. The *"sting"* is gone. The pain is gone. Jesus Christ took that out. Death can threaten us all he wants to, but he cannot hurt those of us who are Christians.

Some day I will see something and see Someone that I have never seen before. There is going to be a voice and a shout, and I will hear it. The Christians who have had their bodies buried six feet below mine will get a head start. When they get to the top of the earth, we will be changed with them, and we will be caught up in the clouds. We will be reunited with loved ones, and we will see Jesus Christ face to face. Thank God He is coming again!

After reading what the Bible says about the Second Coming of Christ, I do not wonder why God said it is *"that blessed hope."*

TRUTHS TO REMEMBER

When we think about Christ's coming for His own, we know that He is our "blessed hope" (Titus 2:13).

Through the Word of God, we find hope (Romans 15:4).

When we really love the Lord, no one will have to plead for us to do what is right. We will do what we are supposed to do out of a heart of love for Jesus Christ (John 14:23; II Corinthians 5:14-15).

God has promised us in His Word that Jesus Christ is coming again (John 14:3; Acts 1:10-11).

Jesus Christ is coming for His own. Every believer will be caught up to be with Him (I Thessalonians 4:16-17).

When Christ comes for His own, He will come secretly and will catch us away in the twinkling of an eye. This is called the Rapture (I Corinthians 15:52).

After Jesus Christ takes every believer to be with Him, there will be a seven-year period on earth called the Tribulation (Daniel 9:24-27; Matthew 24).

During the Tribulation period, the Antichrist will make his appearance on earth. The Tribulation period will conclude with the Battle of Armageddon (Daniel 9:24-27; Revelation 19:11-21).

After the Tribulation period, the Lord Jesus Christ will come in His glory. He will come openly and set up His kingdom on earth. Christ will rule and reign on earth for 1,000 years. This is called the Millennium (Revelation 1:7, 19:11-16, 20:1-6).

Believers who are alive when Jesus Christ comes again will go to heaven without dying (I Corinthians 15:51).

If a Christian dies before the coming of Christ, his soul is set free to be with God immediately. His body will be resurrected at the coming of Christ (II Corinthians 5:8; I Thessalonians 4:13-18).

The resurrected body will be a glorified body, like the body of the Lord Jesus Christ (I Corinthians 15:52-55; I John 3:2).

The greatest day of our lives will be the day we see Jesus Christ (Romans 8:18-23).

When Jesus Christ comes again, there will be a great reunion of all God's children. We will be reunited forever with loved ones and friends who died in the Lord (I Thessalonians 4:13-18).

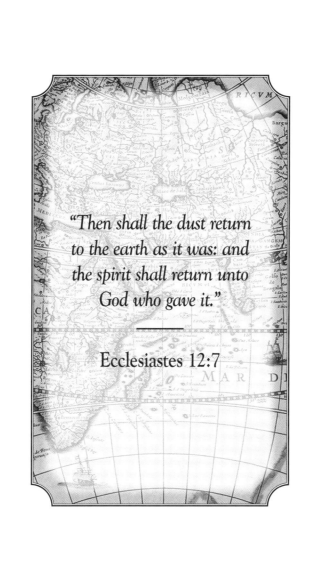

"*Then shall the dust return
to the earth as it was: and
the spirit shall return unto
God who gave it.*"

Ecclesiastes 12:7

WE MUST PREPARE FOR OUR DAY OF DEPARTURE

The ending of the book of Ecclesiastes causes us to think of our day of departure. Chapter twelve is the last chapter of this Old Testament sermon. In verses one through seven of chapter twelve the Bible says,

Remember now thy Creator in the days of thy youth, while the evil days come not, nor the years draw nigh, when thou shalt say, I have no pleasure in them; while the sun, or the light, or the moon, or the stars, be not darkened, nor the clouds return after the rain: in the day when the keepers of the house shall tremble, and the strong men shall bow themselves, and the grinders cease because they are few, and those that look out of the windows be darkened, and the doors shall be shut in the streets, when the sound of the grinding is low, and he shall rise up at the voice of the bird, and all the daughters of musick shall be brought low; also when they shall be afraid of that which is high, and fears shall be in the way, and the almond tree shall flourish, and the grasshopper shall be a burden, and desire shall fail: because man goeth to his long home, and the mourners go about the streets: or ever the silver cord be loosed, or the golden bowl be broken, or the pitcher be broken at the fountain, or the wheel broken at the cistern. Then shall the dust return to the earth as it was: and the spirit shall return unto God who gave it.

The day of our departure is the day we leave this world. Someone has said that the most democratic thing in all the world is death because it comes to all people. The Bible says in Hebrews 9:27, *"And as it is appointed unto men once to die, but after this the judgment."*

The Bible says we shall pass into the presence of God.

All of us who know the Bible and who know the Lord understand that if Jesus Christ does not come soon, we will pass through the door of death. The Bible says we shall pass into the presence of God. Our bodies shall return to the earth and our spirit shall return to God.

I want to live as long as I possibly can, and people are living longer all the time. There are three times as many people in our American population past the age of 60 than there were 100 years ago. An older population now surrounds us. Those who have faithfully walked with God all the years of this earthly journey can be of blessed benefit to the rest of us.

At any given time in America, there are over 12,000 people alive who are past 100 years of age. To think about this is staggering. I want to live to be an old man, but no matter how long I live, I know that at the end of life I shall come to one day that will be my last day. It will be the day of my departure. It may come in the morning, in the evening, or during the night. I do not know when death is coming, but it is coming. We are going to leave this world.

I do not know when death is coming, but it is coming. We are going to leave this world.

It is appropriate that in this book of Ecclesiastes, which is a sermon about life, that the Preacher brings us to think about death in this closing chapter. The Lord desires for us to think about the day of our departure and what we are going to do with Him while we live.

When the Lord Jesus Christ was on the earth, He had so much to say about life. He said in Luke 12:15 that *"a man's life consisteth not in the abundance of the things which he possesseth."* This is the message that America needs to hear. Judging by the way most of us pursue things, many of us have the idea that life has everything to do with how much we possess.

As we consider this passage of Scripture in Ecclesiastes, one of the verses that is so well known is the first verse of this twelfth chapter,

> *Remember now thy Creator in the days of thy youth, while the evil days come not, nor the*

years draw nigh, when thou shalt say, I have no pleasure in them.

The Lord takes us from youth to death in a few words. Verse seven says, *"Then shall the dust return to the earth as it was: and the spirit shall return unto God who gave it."*

As we read the word *"dust,"* we are reminded of the Garden of Eden. Let us go back and refresh our memories with the fact that God created us in His image. In Genesis 2:7 the Bible says, *"And the LORD God formed man of the dust of the ground, and breathed into his nostrils the breath of life; and man became a living soul."*

We were formed from the dust of the earth, and when we die our bodies will return to the dust of the earth from which they came.

Where we spend eternity is determined entirely by what we do with the Person of Jesus Christ while we are here in time.

When God breathed into man, he became a living soul. Man became a creature not just for time, but for eternity. Of course, the real man that lives in the body lives forever. We will live as long as God lives, every one of us, either in heaven or in hell. We live a little while on this earth. Then we go through the experience called death and our bodies are placed in the earth, but our souls are set free to go meet God. We go from time into eternity. Where we spend eternity is determined entirely by what we do with the Person of Jesus Christ while we are here in time. Our Lord said, *"I am the way, the truth, and the life: no man cometh unto the Father, but by me"* (John 14:6).

You may be religious. You may believe in God. You may read the Bible or be a member of some religious group, but you must know Jesus Christ as your personal Savior in order for heaven to be your eternal home. You cannot read the Bible and believe the Bible and come to any other conclusion. Jesus Christ is the only way to heaven.

As we think about the dust of the earth from which we were created, consider what God's Word says in Psalm 103:14. *"For he knoweth our frame; he remembereth that we are dust."*

From the day we are born, we are dying and decaying. This frame of dust is heading back to the ground. We need to take the best care we possibly can of the bodies we have because our bodies are the temple of the Holy Spirit. We are not to abuse our bodies in any way. We have only one body in which to serve God. We must take care of it.

THE POTENTIAL OF THE PRESENT

In Ecclesiastes 12, we see some things that can be done now and only now. In Ecclesiastes 12:1-2 the Bible says,

> *Remember now thy Creator in the days of thy youth, while the evil days come not, nor the years draw nigh, when thou shalt say, I have no pleasure in them; while the sun, or the light, or the moon, or the stars, be not darkened, nor the clouds return after the rain.*

The Lord says while there is light and life, before the darkness comes, we are to do with our lives what He desires for us to do. We are to do this now, at this present moment. This is the potential of the present. Everything we do for Jesus Christ must be done in the present. We may plan to do things in the future or have ideas about what we will do someday, but when those days finally come, we are in the present. Every decision I make for God and everything I do with my life, I do in the present. Seize the golden moment–the present.

Many people spend their lives dreaming and planning or mentally escaping in some way to some time in the future. They miss the golden moment God gives them to live. This moment is all we are guaranteed. We have nothing else. I do not mean to sound unkind, but so many people have spoken to me through the years about what they were going to do when they retire, and they never lived to retire. I do not know how many people have talked to me about what they were going to do for God when they got more time, and they never got more time. God allows us to think and plan; however, if we are going to serve God, trust Him, and live for Him, we must make the most of the moment.

> *At times, fear of the future overwhelms us; but God leads us along day by day, moment by moment, step by step.*

The Lord Jesus taught this to His disciples. At times, fear of the future overwhelms us; but God leads us along day by day, moment by moment, step by step. I have wasted too much of my life worrying about the future and complaining about the present. Learn the potential of the present and make the most of each God-given moment. Trust Christ now. Live for Christ now. Lean on Him now. Know Him as your Savior now. Read your Bible now. Pray now. Be faithful to church now. Build a great Christian life and a great Christian home now. Get on your knees with your wife and pray now. Put God's Word in the hearts of your children now. Realize the potential of the present.

We Must Prepare for Our Day of Departure

The Lord Jesus said in Matthew 6:25-34,

> *Therefore I say unto you, Take no thought for your life, what ye shall eat, or what ye shall drink; nor yet for your body, what ye shall put on. Is not the life more than meat, and the body than raiment? Behold the fowls of the air: for they sow not, neither do they reap, nor gather into barns; yet your heavenly Father feedeth them. Are ye not much better than they? Which of you by taking thought can add one cubit unto his stature? And why take ye thought for raiment? Consider the lilies of the field, how they grow; they toil not, neither do they spin: and yet I say unto you, That even Solomon in all his glory was not arrayed like one of these. Wherefore, if God so clothe the grass of the field, which to day is, and to morrow is cast into the oven, shall he not much more clothe you, O ye of little faith? Therefore take no thought, saying, What shall we eat? or, What shall we drink? or, Wherewithal shall we be clothed? (For after all these things do the Gentiles seek:) for your heavenly Father knoweth that ye have need of all these things. But seek ye first the kingdom of God, and his righteousness; and all these things shall be added unto you. Take therefore no thought for the morrow: for the morrow shall take thought for the things of itself. Sufficient unto the day is the evil thereof.*

Do not plan on serving God later; serve Him now. Do not plan on giving to God later; give to Him now.

We read in Matthew 6:34, *"Take therefore no thought for the morrow: for the morrow shall take thought for the things of itself. Sufficient unto the day is the evil thereof."* This last expression in the sixth chapter of Matthew means that there is enough to deal with every day without adding tomorrow's problems to today's living.

If you are twenty years old, thank God that you are twenty and enjoy being twenty. If you are young and married and you do not have everything in the world, thank God for what you do have and enjoy it. If you are opening Mom's old refrigerator, eating off the old table your aunt and uncle gave you, and sitting on an old, broken down, second-hand couch, be happy. You may think that one day you will have a beautiful house full of new furniture. But when you have a new house along with the mortgage payment and many more obligations, you will say, "Wasn't it great back when we had an old broken down couch and that old refrigerator and table?"

I have not lived as long as some people, but I have lived long enough to know some things. Too many of my "todays" have been wasted worrying about my "tomorrows." There is potential in the present to enjoy life and to be grateful for what I have. Death is coming. Disease is coming. Do not start worrying and fretting because heaven is coming too. Determine that with the help of God you are going to learn to enjoy your life one precious day at a time.

THE PASSING OF OUR YEARS

Nowhere in literature will you find an allegory on aging that can compare to what God gives us here in this passage. He compares the aging process to things we know. He is dealing with the passing of our years. The Bible says in Ecclesiastes 12:3-5,

> *In the day when the keepers of the house shall tremble, and the strong men shall bow themselves, and the grinders cease because they are few, and those that look out of the windows be darkened, and the doors shall be shut in the streets, when the sound of the grinding is low, and he shall rise up at the voice of the bird, and all the daughters of musick shall be brought low; also when they shall be afraid of that which is high, and fears shall be in the way, and the almond tree shall flourish, and the grasshopper shall be a burden, and desire shall fail: because man goeth to his long home, and the mourners go about the streets.*

God uses things with which we are familiar to talk about our decaying bodies. For example, the Bible says in verse three, *"In the day when the keepers of the house shall tremble..."* By *"keepers"* He means our arms and our hands. He goes on to say, *"...and the strong men shall bow themselves, and the grinders cease because they are few..."* The *"strong men"* are our legs. The *"grinders"* are our teeth. The verse says, *"... and those that look out of the windows be darkened..."* This speaks of our eyes. He then says, *"And the doors shall be shut in the streets..."* He is speaking here about our ears and our hearing. He is giving us the story of the passing of our years, the aging process. Look at it.

THE KEEPERS OF THE HOUSE

The Bible says in verse three, *"In the day when the keepers of the house shall tremble."* There was a day when my hands and arms were as steady as can be. I remember growing up around some older people. We played a little game to see who could hold his hands still for the longest period of time. We would try to hold them without moving. Some of the older people, God bless their hearts, just could not do it. Their hands would start to tremble. My dad played this game with us. As children, we could hold a steady hand, but his hands would tremble. If you live long enough, your hands, once so steady and strong, are going to begin to tremble.

THE STRONG MEN

The Bible says, *"The strong men shall bow themselves."* As a boy, I thought that I had the strongest legs in the world. I would

There are many things in life God uses to speak to us and tell us the years are passing.

challenge anyone to a foot race. I discovered that I could run faster than most boys could run. One day I said to my dad, who was crippled, "I would like to race you in a foot race." He never moved quickly anywhere. His old joints were stiff, and he had special shoes made so his feet would not hurt quite as badly. In spite of this, he agreed to run a foot race with me. I have thought of that race many times, and about how badly I beat him in the race because his legs no longer worked properly.

As you notice people whose legs have weakened, remember they were once young, strong, able, and steady. If you live long enough, this will happen to you.

We Must Prepare for Our Day of Departure

The Grinders

I can remember my mother's stepfather saying, "You don't want to get old, your teeth hurt." The Bible says that *"the grinders cease."* Be careful that you do not make fun of the aged. Did you ever eat with anyone who was very careful about what he ate because there were certain things that he could not chew or bite? Young people do not even think about the kinds of things they eat, but later in life *"the grinders cease."*

The Windows Darkened

He then says, *"Those that look out of the windows be darkened."* When you are young, if you do not have eye trouble, you think that you never will have trouble with your eyes. Then one day, you discover that you need glasses.

When I was a boy, my mother would start sewing, and she would call for me by name and ask me to come to her side. She would say, "Honey, can you thread this needle?" As I looked at the great big hole in that needle, I wondered why she could not put that little thread into that great big hole. I would say, "Mama, you mean you can't get that thread in that big hole?" She replied, "I can't see it. Will you help me?" Now, my day has come and yours will come also. My windows are beginning to darken. There are many things in life God uses to speak to us and tell us the years are passing.

The Doors Shut

Then He says, *"And the doors shall be shut in the streets."* Most people who study this passage believe the Lord is making reference to our hearing.

This is an old story of Uncle Buddy Robinson, the tongue-tied Nazarene preacher. He went into the hospital when he was well up in years. The doctors said, "Uncle Buddy, you've lost the hearing in one of your ears." Buddy asked, "What caused it?" The doctor replied, "Old age." Uncle Buddy said, "Well, I can't figure that out. The other ear is as old as that one, and I haven't lost the hearing on that side."

RISING UP AT THE VOICE OF THE BIRD

Solomon continues, *"...when the sound of the grinding is low, and he shall rise up at the voice of the bird..."* He cannot sleep well.

When I was much younger, I could sleep through a storm. Once while we were living in a subdivision, a lady next door to us got the gas pedal stuck on her car as she was entering her garage. She ran the car completely through the garage door and through the exterior brick wall into the yard. The next morning we saw the car sticking out the rear of the house. Fortunately, the lady had not been injured. People from all over the neighborhood were wandering around in her yard. Some of the neighbors said it sounded like an explosion. When the unfortunate lady saw me, she said, "Reverend, didn't you hear it?" I said, "No ma'am, I slept right through it." My sleep is no longer that sound.

Years ago, when I heard older people talk about getting only three or four hours of sleep during the night, I would say, "You mean you don't sleep all the way through the night?" This, too, indicates the passing of years.

Fear of Heights

He then says, *"... when they shall be afraid of that which is high..."*

He is speaking of being afraid of heights. When I was a boy growing up, I thought that every tree was planted for me to climb. There was not a tree in my community that I did not climb. I fell out of some of them too. I certainly do not enjoy that kind of thing now.

Fear in the Way

The Bible goes on to say, *"...and fears shall be in the way..."* My children try to hurry when they are leaving home because I give them a six-point lecture on safety. They know I am going to say, "Be careful how you drive. Fasten that child in his seat. Watch when you're backing out into the street," and a number of other safety tips. You do not think about these things when you are a child, but as you age, the fear of many things starts to loom before you.

The Almond Tree

The Word of God says, *"...and the almond tree shall flourish..."* The almond tree had a beautiful silver color during fruit bearing. He is talking here about the greying of the hair.

Mourners in the Streets

He says, *"...the grasshopper shall be a burden, and desire shall fail: because man goeth to his long home, and the mourners go about the streets..."*

The mourners are waiting for someone to die. In Eastern cultures, there were people who were paid to mourn. They would stand around waiting for someone to die because they wanted a job to mourn. They would go through the streets crying and wailing. When the mourners are *"about the streets,"* someone is near to going home. What a picture is painted by these words.

> *We need to realize the potential of the present, and we need to see afresh and anew the passing of our years in order to make our years count for God.*

Let me tell you what my mother told me. The longer you live the faster life passes by. She said, "Honey, just wait until you go through the thirties." I have been through them. She said, "They go faster than the twenties. And wait until you get in the forties." I had hardly touched the ground in the forties, when they started clicking off like miles on an odometer.

Before long, the mourners are waiting outside. We need to realize the potential of the present, and we need to see afresh and anew the passing of our years in order to make our years count for God.

THE PREPARATION FOR ETERNITY

The Bible says in verse six, *"Or ever the silver cord be loosed..."* This is just a beautiful way of saying that the rope breaks on a bucket or a bowl. The cord is called *"silver"* here. The rope breaks and is gone, and you cannot retrieve it.

WE MUST PREPARE FOR OUR DAY OF DEPARTURE

The entire verse says, *"Or ever the silver cord be loosed, or the golden bowl be broken, or the pitcher be broken at the fountain, or the wheel broken at the cistern."*

There is coming a day when the cord of life will be severed. The mind ceases to work, the heart stops beating, the body is separated from the soul, and you go to meet God. Friends, we need to prepare for eternity. The only way to do it is to realize that there is a real heaven and a real hell. The Lord Jesus came from heaven to keep us from going to hell. He bled and died on the cross of Calvary. He paid our sin debt and was buried and rose from the dead. If we ask Him by faith to forgive our sin and we trust Him as our Savior, He promised He would hear our prayer and forgive our sin and save us. I have claimed that promise. He is my Savior.

When I was a teenage boy, God came to me. Someone witnessed to me about the Lord and showed me how to be saved. How grateful I am for what happened. Not only did I prepare for eternity when I asked the Lord as a young person to forgive my sin and I trusted Jesus Christ as my Savior, but also God enabled me to make more of my life by giving those early years to Him.

> *There is coming a day when the cord of life will be severed. The mind ceases to work, the heart stops beating, the body is separated from the soul, and you go to meet God. Friends, we need to prepare for eternity. The only way to do it is to realize that there is a real heaven and a real hell.*

The greatest thing that you can do is give your life to God while you are young. Not only are you ready for eternity, but you are ready to live. If you did not surrender to God when you were young, the greatest thing to do is give your life to God now. Do not waste another day because the day of our departure is coming sooner than any of us can imagine.

TRUTHS TO REMEMBER

If Jesus Christ does not come soon, all of us will pass through the door of death to meet God (Hebrews 9:27).

We were formed from the dust of the earth. When we die, our bodies will return to the dust of the earth from which they came. We will pass into the presence of God (Genesis 2:7; Ecclesiastes 12:7; II Corinthians 5:8).

Every person will live as long as God lives. Where we spend eternity is determined by what we do with the Person of Jesus Christ now (Genesis 2:7; John 14:6).

We are to live for Jesus Christ now, while we have life and strength to serve Him. We should not plan on serving God later; we should serve Him now (Ecclesiastes 12:1; James 4:14-17).

God's children should not worry over the future. If we do, we will not serve Him as we should today (Matthew 6:25-34).

As we recognize that our bodies are aging, we should be reminded that our day of departure is drawing nigh. We need to prepare for eternity (Ecclesiastes 12:2-7).

The greatest thing we can do with the life God has given us is to give it back to God now. We should not waste another day because our day of departure is coming sooner than any of us can imagine (Ecclesiastes 12:1, 13-14).

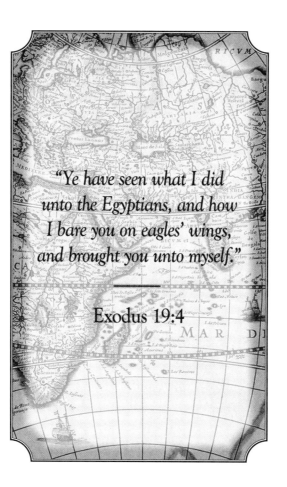

"Ye have seen what I did
unto the Egyptians, and how
I bare you on eagles' wings,
and brought you unto myself."

———

Exodus 19:4

CHAPTER THIRTEEN

GOD BEARS US ON EAGLES' WINGS

We all need to understand how the Lord works in our lives. The Bible says in Exodus 19:3-4, *"And Moses went up unto God, and the LORD called unto him out of the mountain, saying, Thus shalt thou say to the house of Jacob, and tell the children of Israel; ye have seen what I did unto the Egyptians, and how I bare you on eagles' wings, and brought you unto myself."*

THE MEANING OF LIFE

In this passage of Scripture, the Lord gives us the meaning of life. No matter where you look in the Bible, and no matter what people say to you throughout your life, you will never find a better definition for the meaning of life than what we find in the nineteenth chapter of the book of Exodus.

The Bible says that God brought His people unto Himself on eagles' wings. The meaning of life is that God brings us unto Himself. This is what the Lord wants. He wants us to come unto Him. The Lord Jesus Christ said in Matthew 11:28, *"Come unto me, all ye that labour and are heavy laden, and I will give you rest."*

The Lord explained to Moses that when He called him down to Egypt to lead God's people out, He wanted Moses to understand that He was bringing them not to a land, but to a Person.

God said, *"I brought you unto myself."* He wants us to know Him, to come unto Him. This is why, after many years in the ministry, the apostle Paul wrote the church in Philippi in Philippians 3:10, *"That I may know him, and the power of his resurrection, and the fellowship of his sufferings."* Surely Paul knew the Lord as his Savior. He met Him on the Damascus road. After all those years of serving the Lord, he said, "My great goal in life is to know the Lord, to come unto Him."

> *The meaning of life is that God brings us unto Himself.*

The meaning of life is to know the Lord. How well do you know Him? May we come to know Jesus Christ in a way that we have never known Him before, more intimately than we have ever known Him. Let us enter into sweet communion with Him. Christ can do for us what no one else can do for us.

The meaning of life is that the Lord brings us unto Himself. Once we realize this, we should look for Christ in all things, every day, everywhere we go. The Lord wants us to meet Him every day, in everything He does. Look for Him because He is working in all these things to bring us unto Himself. The Bible says in Philippians 2:13, *"For it is God which worketh in you both to will and to do of his good pleasure."*

THE METHOD GOD USES

In Deuteronomy 32, we find the method that God uses to accomplish the meaning of life. This is how God works to bring all this to pass. He says in verses eleven and twelve, *"As an eagle stirreth up her nest, fluttereth over her young, spreadeth abroad her wings, taketh them, beareth them on her wings: so the LORD alone did lead him, and there was no strange god with him."*

The Bible makes it very simple. The Word of God says, *"As an eagle...so the LORD..."* As an eagle works, so does the Lord work. God says, "I want you to understand what I am doing in your life. I want you to know Me. I want you to come unto Me."

This is why Moses said in Psalm 90:1-2, *"LORD thou hast been our dwelling place...from everlasting to everlasting, thou art God."* Moses

Look for Him, because He is working in all these things to bring us unto Himself.

learned this great lesson when his mother by faith placed him in a basket among the bulrushes. He was not on the river's brink; he was in the hands of God. Moses learned this when Pharaoh's daughter found him and took him to Pharaoh's palace. He was not in Pharaoh's palace; he was in the hands of God. He learned this as he grew up in the palace of Pharaoh and was trained in all the wonders of Egypt. He was not there as the child of Pharaoh; he was in the hands of God. As a forty-year-old man, after he had tried to take things into his own hands to deliver his people, fled for his life to the backside of the desert, and stayed there for forty years, Moses learned that he was not just in a desert place; he was in the hands of God.

As an old man, Moses could see that God had been in everything that had happened to him. The Lord had led him, protected him, cared for him, and brought him to the present hour. In this passage, God reminded him that all of this happened in order to bring Moses unto Himself.

AS AN EAGLE, SO THE LORD BUILDS

The Lord says, "The way the eagle works is the way that I am going to work." *"As an eagle...so the LORD..."* As an eagle builds, so the Lord builds.

Far off, in some rocky place, high above the ground, the eagle finds the perfect location in which to build the nest. The greatest of care is taken in building that nest, gathering branches and other things from the earth and carrying them to the nest to make it just exactly like it needs to be. The nest is prepared with tender, loving care.

This is a building process that goes on. The life of the eagle cannot continue unless the building process goes on. As the eagle builds, so the Lord builds. Sometimes we hear the expression "self-made people." But God builds His people.

Often I am asked, "How long does it take you to prepare a sermon?" It takes my entire life to prepare every sermon I preach because everything that has ever happened in my life is a part of what I am today. Every little tributary that is emptied into the river of my existence is what makes me what I am in this day and hour. God is building us and He is not finished yet. God's Word says in Philippians 1:6, *"Being confident of this very thing, that he which hath begun a good work in you will perform it until the day of Jesus Christ."* We know He will finish because someday we are going to be like the Lord Jesus. Thank God for that.

The Lord saved me from where I was, right where He found me; and if someday I am going to be like the Lord Jesus, I am going to be one continual construction site until I see the Son of God. He is still working.

If you see on your construction site something He has not quite finished, keep in mind that God is still working on His children as long as His children are walking as His servants on this earth.

God is building us and He is not finished yet.

When the disciples of our Lord went to the coasts of Caesarea Philippi, the Bible says that the Lord Jesus had a question and answer session with them. He said in Matthew 16:13-18,

> *Whom do men say that I the Son of man am? And they said, Some say that thou art John the Baptist: some, Elias; and others, Jeremias, or one of the prophets. He saith unto them, But whom say ye that I am? And Simon Peter answered and said, Thou art the Christ, the Son of the living God. And Jesus answered and said unto him, Blessed art thou, Simon Bar-jona: for flesh and blood hath not revealed it unto thee, but my Father which is in heaven. And I say also unto thee, That thou art Peter, and upon this rock I will build my church; and the gates of hell shall not prevail against it.*

The Lord is the One who builds His church. We must allow Him to do the building. As an eagle, so the Lord builds.

AS AN EAGLE, SO THE LORD BREAKS

As an eagle, so the Lord breaks. *"As an eagle stirreth up her nest..."* God works like an eagle. Mother knows that baby eaglets were not born to stay in a nest for the rest of their lives. She cares for them and she longs to be near them. She is proud of them, but they were not born to stay in the nest, so she must do something that is painful to do.

She worked so hard building that nest, but she must begin to remove some of the soft things that made it so comfortable. Some of the sticks that had been lying horizontally to make it comfortable for them are now turned vertically.

God is in disturbances just as much as He is in deliverances.

If we could hear the little eaglets talking in the nest, they would say something like, "It is impossible to find a comfortable place around here! Ouch! That hurts! I can't find a place to sit. I don't know what is going on. Everything was perfect until just a few days ago. Something went wrong." This mother eagle is causing her eaglets to look beyond the nest, making them realize they must get out of there. She must break up the nest.

God is in disturbances just as much as He is in deliverances. Every one of us is exactly the way we are for one reason. We are content to be that way. Some folks are so content that they would just sit where they are and do no more until the Lord Jesus comes. We must realize that God wants to stir us up.

We wonder why things happen. You may wonder why you are having difficulty. You may wonder why things are not going smoothly for you. It is because God wants to do more with your life than He has ever done before.

When I was saved, I was placed in the body of Christ by the Spirit of God by the baptism of the Holy Spirit. A fellow asked me recently while I was out visiting if I had been baptized by the Spirit of God. I said, "I certainly have. When I was saved, I was baptized by the Spirit of God and placed in the body of Christ."

He breaks up things in my life to cause me to seek Him.

I am indwelt by the Holy Spirit. The Lord came to live in me at the moment of salvation, but I am to be filled daily by the Holy Spirit. I am sealed by the Spirit of God unto the day of redemption. I have the earnest of the Holy Spirit. I received gifts of the Holy Spirit when I got saved, and I can have the fruit of the Holy Spirit as I abide in Christ and the Holy Spirit works in my life.

I believe that for every task God gives us, He anoints us with His Holy Spirit to do that job. God has anointed me to be the pastor of the church I presently pastor. I have that confidence, not in my ability, but in the fact that God Almighty has called me and has anointed me to be the pastor of this church. Surely, if the Lord has put me here, then the Lord's anointing will be upon me to do what He wants me to do. The Lord has equipped me to pastor. He breaks up things in my life to cause me to seek Him. Remember the meaning of life is to come to the Lord.

AS AN EAGLE, SO THE LORD BROODS

When we are having problems and difficulties, we wonder, "Where is God in all of this?" I know what it is like to deal with problems. I do not enjoy them, but I thank God for what I can learn from them. The greatest thing I learn from them is that Christ will see me through.

Our heavenly Father broods over us. The Bible says in Deuteronomy 32:11, *"As an eagle stirreth up her nest, fluttereth over her young..."* Up in the nest, the eaglet is watching as mother eagle does something beautiful and majestic. She has already stirred up the nest and made the eaglets uncomfortable. She has their attention. Very few times in our lives does God really get our attention. When He gets our attention, we should respond to Him. Some people may go for years without God getting their attention, but when He gets it, they should respond to Him. Mother eagle has their attention. They are no longer comfortable in the nest. Suddenly, they see her. Beautifully, majestically, she glides through the air. Those gorgeous wings are spread as she moves through the air with the eaglets in view.

Very few times in our lives does God really get our attention.

She watches them because she has walked that path before and she knows what is going on inside their little hearts. They are looking at her and thinking, "Could I ever do that? Could I ever fly like that? Mother looks like me, and I look like her. Mother is out of the nest, and I am in the nest. Could I ever get out of this nest and do something I have never done before?" Eaglets do not learn to fly by watching one another. They learn to fly by watching their mother. Christians never grow by watching one another. They grow by looking to Jesus Christ.

There are disappointing, heartbreaking things that happen sometimes to turn our eyes back on the Son of God. The beauty of it is that His eyes are always on us. In the darkest night, the roughest time, the loneliest hour, when it seems as though it would be easier to die than live, God is watching you, brooding over you. He is always tenderly, lovingly looking at you. The Bible says that we are never alone and never forsaken.

As an Eagle, So the Lord Bears

Mother has a big job on her hands because one of those little eaglets has to be the first one out of the nest. The first eaglet walks over until there is nothing to stand on—it is all air! Once he gets over the edge, he must fly. As these eaglets watch their mother, beating within their breast is a desire to do what she is doing. Suddenly, over the nest one comes. Fluttering his wings as rapidly as possible, he tries to fly. He makes it for a moment, then suddenly, his mother sees him faltering. Like a rocket, she zooms down beneath him, spreads abroad her great wings, and catches him. She bears him on her mighty wings and takes him heavenward, higher and higher, until she removes her wings and lets him try again.

The Bible says in verse eleven, *"As an eagle stirreth up her nest, fluttereth over her young, spreadeth abroad her wings, taketh them, beareth them on her wings."* She makes sure that he does what he is supposed to do. He must exercise faith to fly. He was born to fly, not to sit in a nest.

Many Christians have never realized why they were born again. We were not born again to sit in a church house. We were not born again to build buildings. We were not born again to have meetings. We were born again to abide in Christ and to tell others about the Son of God. We fail, but when we are failing and falling, our heavenly Father is there to bear us on His wings.

I have thought many times that I could not live and would not live, but God saw me through. I could only fall so far until I fell on His wings.

The little eaglet tries again and the mother eagle sees that his wings are faltering. Again, like a rocket, she zooms down beneath him, picks him up, carries him heavenward, moves her wings, and lets him try again. Finally he flies!

In all of the recorded studies of eagles, researchers have never found that even one eaglet has fallen to his death because he was not caught on his mother's wings. I know that I am safe in Jesus Christ. I am sure of heaven. I have the promise that the Lord will take care of me.

God said, "Moses, I want you to understand something. The meaning of life is that I bring you to Myself." I want you to know the Savior. I want you to see that everything He does, He does to get our attention, to bring us unto Himself. This is the way the Lord works.

First of all, He builds. Then He has to stir us up; He breaks. He is always brooding, always watching over us. When we attempt things for Him, remember that if we do fail, He will bear us on His blessed wings.

TRUTHS TO REMEMBER

The meaning of life is that the Lord brings us unto Himself. God desires for us to know Him and to enter into sweet communion with Him (Exodus 19:4; Matthew 11:28; Philippians 3:10).

God is working in all things to bring us unto Himself (Exodus 19:4; Philippians 2:13).

God will continue working in the lives of His children as long as we are living on this earth. We know He will finish His work because one day we will be like the Lord Jesus (Philippians 1:6; I John 3:2).

God is in disturbances just as much as He is in deliverances. The Lord breaks up things in our lives to cause us to seek Him (Deuteronomy 32:11-12; Romans 8:28; Psalm 61:1-4).

We grow as Christians, not by looking at one another, but by looking to Jesus Christ (Hebrews 12:2).

In the darkest night, the roughest time, and the loneliest hour, God is always watching over us. He will never leave us nor forsake us (Hebrews 13:5).

We were born again to abide in Christ and to tell others about the Son of God (John 15:4,16; Revelation 4:11).

God's Word promises that we are safe in Jesus Christ. If we fail, He will bear us up on His wings (Deuteronomy 32:11-12; Romans 8:31).

Sunday School materials are available for use in conjunction with *Truths Every Christian Needs to Know.* For a complete listing of available materials from Crown Christian Publications, please call 1-877 AT CROWN, or write to: P.O. Box 159 ❖ Powell, TN ❖ 37849

Visit us on the Web at FaithfortheFamily.com
"A Website for the Christian Family"

CROWN
CHRISTIAN
PUBLICATIONS
Royal Reading

ABOUT THE AUTHOR

Clarence Sexton is the pastor of the Temple Baptist Church and founder of Crown College in Knoxville, Tennessee. He has written more than twenty books and booklets. He speaks in conferences throughout the United States and has conducted training sessions for pastors and Christian workers in several countries around the world. He and his wife, Evelyn, have been married for thirty-six years. They have two grown sons and six grandchildren. For more information about the ministry of Clarence Sexton, visit our website at www.FaithfortheFamily.com.

OTHER HELPFUL BOOKS BY CLARENCE SEXTON:

THE LORD IS MY SHEPHERD

EARNESTLY CONTEND
   FOR THE FAITH

THE CHRISTIAN HOME

TRUTHS EVERY
   CHRISTIAN NEEDS TO KNOW

LORD, SEND A REVIVAL

THE PARABLES OF JESUS
   VOLUME 1

ISSUES OF LIFE ANSWERED
   FROM THE BIBLE

THE CONCLUSION OF THE
   WHOLE MATTER VOLUME 1

THE PARABLES OF JESUS
   VOLUME 2

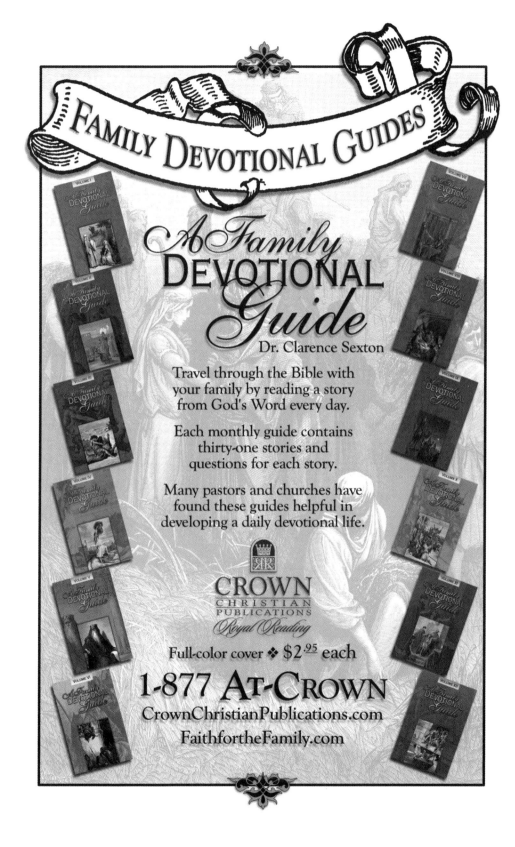